Ármin Vámbéry

The Coming Struggle for India

Ármin Vámbéry

The Coming Struggle for India

ISBN/EAN: 9783744693417

Printed in Europe, USA, Canada, Australia, Japan

Cover: Foto ©ninafisch / pixelio.de

More available books at **www.hansebooks.com**

THE COMING

STRUGGLE FOR INDIA.

BEING AN ACCOUNT OF

*THE ENCROACHMENTS OF RUSSIA IN CENTRAL ASIA, AND OF THE
DIFFICULTIES SURE TO ARISE THEREFROM TO ENGLAND.*

BY

ARMINIUS VAMBÉRY.

————◆●◆————

CASSELL & COMPANY, LIMITED:
LONDON, PARIS, NEW YORK & MELBOURNE.

1885.

To

RUSSELL SHAW, Esq.

BUDA PESTH UNIVERSITY,
July 2, 1885.

MY DEAR MR. SHAW,

You are a Liberal in your political views; I found you liberal in the hospitality you have bestowed on me; and I hope you will be liberal in judging these pages, which I dedicate to you.

In other countries an author would have hardly ventured to dedicate to his friend of Liberal persuasion a book containing a strong criticism upon the policy of the Liberal party. But in England fair play is fully admitted in political opinions, even if they come from a foreigner. This is a fact, of which I have had ample opportunity to convince myself during my late lecturing tour in your country; and it is the substance of the various addresses which I then delivered, that I offer now to the public in the present book form.

Believe me,

Dear Mr. Shaw,

Yours sincerely,

A. VAMBÉRY.

CONTENTS.

THE COMING
STRUGGLE FOR INDIA.

CHAPTER I.

THE WAY TO TASHKEND.

GREAT events are casting their shadows before them; the unmistakable signs of historic revolutions silently progressing are thickening around us; and if, nevertheless, we refuse to give credence to facts irrevocably accomplished and full of significance, it must be ascribed not to the dulness of our senses, but to the prevailing rigidly conservative character of the great majority of politicians.

The rivalry between Russia and England must have become evident from the very moment when Spain, Portugal, Holland, and France, gradually disappeared from the field of conquests in Asia, and when that old mother-country was left open to the ambition of the first mentioned two great nations. England, entering into the arena of conquest from

B

the south, had slowly but constantly worked her way
through India, until out of the small trading Company
had grown a mighty empire; an empire founded upon
the heroism, patriotism, and lust of adventure of
those islanders, who, feeling themselves somewhat
cramped in their narrow insular home, had started to
the distant East in order to satisfy their curiosity, to
couple their names with some glorious deed in the
cause of humanity, and to reflect honour upon their
own mother-country.

At the outset nobody knew the ultimate border of
the new acquisition. Conquests necessitated fresh and
new conquests, and when the State supplanted the
simple trading Company, the Indian acquisition was
as extensive as any of the former Mogul or Hindoo
Rajahs had ever been able to unite under his
sceptre. The conquest of India was and is undoubtedly the glory of our western civilisation; it
is the best mark of the superiority of our indomitable
European spirit, and of the strength of young Europe
compared with old and crumbling Asia.

As to Russia, the causes and the course of her
conquests were of quite a different nature. The
whole structure of the Russian empire rests exclusively
upon conquests and annexation; for it must be borne
in mind that Russia is not an ethnical but a political
nation. The Russians were at the beginning only a

small number of Slavs, grafted upon Ugrian, Turko-
Tartar, and Finnic elements, but which in the course
of time gradually enlarged, and would have had
already a pre-eminent part in the historical events of
the Middle Ages, if temporary revolutions and wars,
produced by Asiatic conquerors, had not interfered,
and delayed the growth of the national body. Among
these drawbacks we reckon the irruption of the Mongols under Djenghis Khan, and the great war under
Timur, both of them historical events which crippled
and maimed the Grand-Duchy of Muscovy ; but in the
end Russian society, imbued with the spirit of
Christian civilisation, nevertheless triumphed over the
rude and barbarian representatives of Asia. The
Golden Horde crumbled to pieces, the empire of Timur
was scattered to the winds; and victorious Russia, by
annexing one portion after another, not only found
herself succeeding to the heritage of her Asiatic predecessors, but also possessing the best means of
continuing in the path of ulterior conquests, and of
consolidating her new acquisitions in a way quite
superior to the means and modes at the disposal of
Asiatic despots.

After having subdued the middle and lower
Volga, Russia turned her attention partly to the East,
partly to the West. In both directions she earned
unexpected success. In the East she appeared as the

B 2

representative of Europe two centuries ago, and, armed with the superior arms of that time, she managed to conquer vast multitudes with a comparatively small number of men. Siberia was conquered in the sixteenth century, and when Kutchum Khan, after having been defeated by the daring troopers under the lead of Yermak, armed with firearms, and losing his crown and empire, was asked to surrender, the old blind man, discovered in the midst of the woods, said : " I am blind, deaf, poor and deserted, but I do not complain about the loss of my treasures, I only grieve that the Russians have taken captive my dear child, my son Asmanak. If I had him with me I should willingly renounce my crown, my riches, all my other wives and remaining children. Now I shall send my family to Bokhara, and I myself shall go to the Nogais. I did not go to the Czar in my more prosperous days, when I was rich and mighty ; shall I go now in order to meet with a shameful death."

From the eastern Tartars in Siberia, Russia turned to the western Tartars in the Crimea, to those very Nogais with whom Kutchum Khan expected to find a shelter. Here the sway of the Sultan of Turkey had become loosened at that time, and the Empress Catherine plucked fresh laurels for her crown after a hard struggle, which sealed the fate of the Khans of Bagtche-Sarai for ever. From the Isker in Siberia to the banks of the Pruth, all became Russian. The various populations had to undergo the process of Russification, and the newly annexed elements had hardly been incorporated into the body of Muscovitism, when the progress towards the south already began, and the subjugation of the Kirghis steppes was already initiated.

That is the real outset of the Russian conquests in Central Asia.

It was a hard nut Russia had to crack here, a task arduous beyond measure; for besides the struggle to be fought with men, she met with a serious obstacle in nature, through the endless barren steppes, varying with hard clay, sand many feet deep, and wide waterless tracts of country. Any other Government would have been afraid to engage in that undertaking; but despotic Russia, unchecked in the waste of men and money, entered upon it with the determination of overcoming all obstacles. The steppes were attacked from two different sides, from the east and the west. As to the eastern route, Siberia formed the basis, and down glided the Russian Cossacks from the Altai, along the western border of China to the lake of Issyk Kul, as smoothly and quietly as the Russian outposts succeeded in skirting the western frontier of the Kirghis country from the Lesser Horde to the Aral lake and to the Yaxartes. It was the work of two centuries, accomplished in a wonderful way, with that characteristic Muscovite tenacity, cunning, and recklessness, which have wrought so many wonders and surprises to the western world.

The Kirghises, numbering beyond three millions of souls, and representing the prototype of Turkish nomadic society, offered from the beginning that special mode of resistance we encounter in the case of the nomads of Asia and America. At first a few influential chieftains were enticed by bribes, presents, and imaginary distinctions, assisted as usual by the generously offered flask of *rodki*. Of course, the allegiance thus obtained was of no avail and no duration, for no sooner had the Russian *tchinovnik* disappeared from the scene of his action, than the Kirghis chief forgot his oath of fidelity, as well as the rich presents he had received from the White Padishah of the Neva. Russia had to resort to other means. She built on various points small forts, originally intended to harbour the merchants on their way to the steppe ; for the Czar is a benignant ruler, who is anxious that his subjects should be provided with all the necessaries of life, and he even went so far as to build mosques and Mohammedan colleges for the pious Kirghises, an act which has been very frequently rebuked as impolitic and unwise. This paternal care, however, did not bear the expected fruit ; the so-called halting places for Russian traders were soon turned into small forts, garrisoned by soldiers; from the walls of which loopholes for cannon looked far into the desert, and overawed the restless nomads more than any imperial ukase, written with gold ink, and all the sacred oaths of the chieftains sworn upon the Koran had done. By extending this line of fortifications into the country of the Kirghises, Russia succeeded in thrusting a formidable wedge into the body of her adversary. Disunion amongst the Kirghises did the rest, and in spite of temporary risings, Russia could safely assert soon after the Crimean war that she had become the undisputed master of the whole Kirghis country as far as the right bank of the Yaxartes, including the Aral Sea, where her operations by land were supported by a small flotilla.

While these large operations were going on, Europe, always happy to engage Russia in Asia and to keep her off from European politics, cared but very little for the doings of the northern colossus in this outlying part of the eastern world. But little oozed out concerning these new conquests, and that little generally came through the channel of European travellers, *savants*, delighted at the warm reception they got from Russian officials, and full of praises of the humanitarian work Russia was doing in those outlying barbarous countries, where

every step was accompanied by the civilisation of the
West, and where every flash of cannon was said to be a
new rising sun of our European culture. Happy
delusion for our careless diplomatists! But still
happier means for aggressive Russia, and but for these
treacherous lights beginning to throw a rather dubious
reflex beyond the Suleiman range, our blissful Europe
would still send fervent prayers to heaven for the
civilising columns of holy Russia, as the imbecility
of our diplomatists continues to do to this very
day.

England, justly disquieted by the Russian move
towards Khiva, had found it advisable to try whether
any diplomatic transactions with the three khanates
of Turkestan could not produce such an effect as to
stop the Russian progress. Lord Auckland imagined,
that by calling the attention of the rulers of the
three khanates to the impending danger, a union
might be effected which would prove a barrier against
Russia. This was the origin of the mission of the
late Sir Alexander Burnes, an accomplished young
Scotchman, who was well received at the Court of
Nasrullah Khan, the father of the present Emir of
Bokhara. His transactions secured to England a
treaty of commerce; they produced also relations of
amity between Bokhara and India; but neither
Khokand nor Khiva could this clever diplomatist

visit, and no sooner had he returned to Europe than, with the death of the chief minister at Nasrullah, the effect of the happy journey vanished, and Bokhara remained as before, utterly heedless of coming events, and continuing, as before, to weaken the neighbouring States instead of giving them strength and support against the approaching danger.

Russia, at the same time, was not slow to counteract this stroke of policy by a similar approach to England's nearest neighbour, namely, Afghanistan. First of all, she began to meddle with Herat through the intermediary of the King of Persia, whom she made her involuntary ally after the treaty of Turkman-chai. The King of all Kings of Iran, a sickly man, had, together with his half-crazy minister, for a long time back cherished the idea of re-conquering the large dominions of Shah Abbas the Great. The Keyanian Cap, representing the Crown of Persia, looking shabby and worn out, was sadly wanting in new jewels. Wooden guns inlaid with brass were soon got ready ; and Count Simonitch, the Russian ambassador, had only to stir the fire to bring the Persian army, a crowd of beggars clad in rags, before the walls of Herat. Fortunately England, aware of the imminent danger, selected the proper man to frustrate the machinations of her rival—Eldred Pottinger, an English officer of

rare talents. One man alone was sufficient to anni-
hilate all the grandiloquent schemes of Persia. The
fire of the wooden guns had no effect; the balls hewn
of marble, invented by the ingenious Persian prime
minister, were smashed to pieces on the walls erected
under the lead of the clever and brave Englishman.
The Shah got the dysentery instead of laurels, and
the half-emaciated and decimated army of the King
of all Kings, together with their Russian advisers,
returned to Teheran. Herat was made secure once
more against the immediate attack of Russia.

Whilst this was going on, a young Russian officer
of Polish extraction, named Vitkovitch, had to per-
form at Kabul, at Dost Mohammed Khan's, the same
part which Sir Alexander Burnes had so cleverly
played at Bokhara. In the "Memoirs of the late
General Blaramberg," a German officer in the Russian
service, we read, among other interesting details
regarding the Russian doings in Herat and Kabul,
how Alexander von Humboldt had met with a young
Polish gentleman exiled to Siberia, and how this
young man, of high education and refined manners,
succeeded in gaining the sympathies of the great
German scholar to such an extent that he interceded
in his favour with the Emperor Nicholas the First,
and obtained his pardon from the Czar on the condition of the gifted young Pole's entering the

Russian service and devoting his abilities to Russian interests. This young Polish gentleman was the afterwards famous Russian secret agent, M. Vitkovitch, at Kabul. A great linguist, fully versed in the way of dealing with Asiatics, and therefore a competent rival of Sir Alexander Burnes, he had to gain over the sympathies of Dost Mohammed Khan for the Court of St. Petersburg.

As the last named Afghan prince failed in his endeavour to secure British assistance for the re-occupation of Peshawur, then in the hands of Rendjit Singh, he very naturally lent an eager ear to overtures coming from the rival of Great Britain. Vitkovitch was listened to with particular attention; but owing to the great distance Russian outposts then stood from Afghanistan, all that the Envoy could afford to give at that time consisted in empty promises, totally inadequate to satisfy the astute grey-wolf of Afghanistan. The transaction, therefore, turned out an empty bubble. Vitkovitch returned to St. Petersburg *re male gesta*, and being disavowed by his Government, the unfortunate young man committed suicide in the very blossom of his life. Thus are things in Russia. Successful generals and diplomatists, publicly declared to have acted against the will of the Czar, are not only acknowledged, but rewarded; whilst those who remain unsuccessful are rebuked, and have to pay the penalty of death for Russian disgrace.

As to Afghanistan, the sulky attitude of Dost Mohammed Khan towards England very soon became the cause of the first Afghan war, in which England spent many thousands of lives and over £20,000,000 of money. Kabul and Kandahar were taken, but had to be evacuated; and the disastrous failure, owing not so much to the want of military valour of the British soldiers, but rather to the utter want of knowledge how to deal with Asiatics, imparted the first stain of shame to the English military character in Asia. It is exceedingly interesting to notice how all the personal valour and courage, all the heroic self-immolation, rare circumspection, and ability of single individuals, are rendered of no avail by the short-sightedness of leading politicians, of wavering statesmen, and of an irresolute Government. The news of the English defeat in Afghanistan spread all over Central Asia, and was the first deadly blow to the *prestige* of Great Britain in the East. The Khans, Emirs, and Begs exulted with joy over the victory of their co-religionists, the Afghans. Mohammedan barbarism thought itself again safe against the threatening attacks of our western culture, and in delusive blissfulness quite overlooked the black clouds gathering in the north

—clouds which cast their gloomy shadows, even at that time, as far as the banks of the Yaxartes, and were fraught with those unmistakable signs that prognosticated the devastating tempest sweeping over Central Asia two decades later.

CHAPTER II.

RUSSIA, after having subdued the Kirghises; and reached, on the left bank of the Yaxartes, the outlying northern districts of Khokand, had in the meantime fully prepared all the ways and means of an attack upon the three khanates. During my stay in Bokhara in 1863, I heard vague rumours only of the Russian approach towards Tashkend. "The formerly sweet waters of the Yaxartes river," said a pious Mohammedan to me, "have been utterly spoiled and rendered undrinkable, for the Russians have watered their horses and dipped their abominable idols into it; but as to the country of Khokand, they will never be able to conquer it, for the glorious spirit of the holy Khodja Ahmed Yessevi at Hazreti-Turkestan is on the watch, and will never allow the infidels to pass into the region of Islam." Unhappy dreamer! He and his countrymen had quite forgotten that the poor Khodja Ahmed Yessevi was but a doubtful champion against the adventurous General Tchernayeff, who, with but two thousand men, not only trampled upon the grave of the said saint, but succeeded also in capturing Tashkend, the great commercial centre of the north of the khanates in 1864, and defeating an enemy at least twenty times as numerous as his daring companions in arms.

It was during the very year I arrived in London that the news of the capture of Tashkend had reached Europe. A few weeks before that I happened to meet Lord Palmerston, and I consider it no small distinction to have been listened to with attention by this greatest English statesman of modern times. After having given to him the outlines of my stirring adventures, and related all that I had heard of the approach of Russia, adding, at the same time, remarks upon the comparative case with which the Muscovite would advance towards the Oxus, the noble lord said amongst other things, that we Hungarians, like the Poles, had a hot brain, and that many generations must pass before Russia would be able to pull down the Tartar barrier and approach the country intervening between India and Bokhara. I very much doubt whether the great English statesman seriously meant what he stated to me, for his careful inquiries into sundry details belied his seeming indifference. At all events he did not continue with that Olympian calmness with which he had tried to impress me at first, and shared by no means in the indifference exhibited by English statesmen I occasionally met after the publication of the Russian circular of Prince Gortschakoff in 1864. It must be borne in mind that Russia, fully conscious of the importance of the step she had taken, condescended to give explanations even without being asked. The aforesaid circular, intended to appease any eventual anxiety, related in a cleverly written memorandum how the Government of the Czar had been compelled, against his own will and without any hope of material benefit, to annex the country of the Kirghises; and how these Kirghises, unruly fellows, could be only governed and ruled from a point where the cultivable region might secure a firm footing for the invader, and afford the best opportunity to check disorder and lawlessness.

In that famous circular it was said that the following reasons had mainly precipitated the conquest of Tashkend :—

"1. It has been deemed indispensable that the two fortified lines of our frontiers, one starting from China and extending as far as the Issyk Kul lake, the other from the Aral Sea along the Syr-Darya, should be united by fortified points, in such a manner that all our posts would be in a condition to eventually sustain each other, and not to allow any interval to remain open through which the nomadic tribes might effect with impunity their invasions and depredations.

" 2. It was essential that the line of our advanced forts laid down in this manner should be situated in a country not only sufficiently fertile to secure their provisions, but also to facilitate regular colonisation, for this alone can secure to an occupied country a future of stability and prosperity in winning the neighbouring populations for civilised life.

" 3. Lastly, it was urgent to fix that line in a definite manner, in order to escape from *the dangerous and almost inevitable inducements to go on from repression to reprisals, which might result in an endless extension.*"

" With this object the basis of a system had to be laid down, which should be founded not only upon reason, which is elastic, *but upon geographical and political conditions which are of a fixed and permanent nature.*"

In reading these passages we really are at a loss to decide whether grim humour or unprecedented hypocrisy and impudence have dictated them. The ink was scarcely dry with which the lines had been written, when Russia, anxious to avoid " endless extension," plunged again into fresh conquests. Khudayar Khan, the ruler of Khokand, a noted coward even in Central Asia, had soon lost his spirits, and implored Muzaffar-ed-din-Khan for assistance. Bokhara, reputed at that time the very stronghold of

c

moral and material strength in Central Asia, was soon at hand with an army outnumbering the Russian adventurers ten or fifteen times; an army in name only, but consisting chiefly of a rabble, ill-armed, and devoid of any military qualities. By dint of preponderating numbers, the Bokhariots succeeded so far as to inflict a loss upon the daring Russian general at Irdjar, who, constrained to retreat upon Tashkend, was at once deposed by his superiors in St. Petersburg, and instead of praises being bestowed upon him for the capture of Tashkend, he had to feel the weight of Russian ingratitude. His successor, General Romanovsky, played the part of a consolidator and a preparer, and as soon as this duty was fulfilled he likewise was superseded by General Kauffmann, a German from the Baltic Russian provinces, uniting the qualities of his predecessors in one person, and doing accordingly the work entrusted to him with pluck and luck in a comparatively short time. In 1868 the whole Yaxartes valley, together with Samarkand, the former capital of Timur, fell into the hands of Russia, and General Kauffmann would have proceeded to Bokhara, and even farther, if Muzaffar-ed-din-Khan, terrified by the heavy blows which he had received, and afraid of a revolutionary rising in his own country headed by his own son, had not voluntarily submitted and begged for peace.

At the treaty of Serpul, the Emir was granted the free possession of the country which was left to him, beginning beyond Kermineh, as far as Tchardjui in the south ; and not only was he promised vigorous support in all his possessions beyond the Oxus, but Russian friendship even went so far as to suppress for him a rebellion which had broken out at Shehri Sebz, and amity seemed to spring up between these two formerly implacable enemies. Of course the Emir had to pledge himself to be a true and faithful ally of Russia. He had to pay the heavy war indemnity, including all the robberies and embezzlements of Russian officers ; he had to place his sons under the tutorship of the Czar in order to be brought up at St. Petersburg, in the very centre of the blackest infidelity ; and ultimately he had to cede three points on his southern frontier—namely, Djam, Kerki, and Tchardjui, in order to secure a starting point for Russia towards the south in case of necessity. All these were certainly most oppressive burdens ; but what on earth would not the Emir have given to save the shadow of his sovereignty ? Of course Russia was very wise to leave him in the delusive dream of his independence ; for besides the heavy costs involved by immediate annexation, the administration of the country by Russian officials would have proved a useless expense to the exchequer. This abstemious policy had borne

c 2

its fruits—for Russia not only gained the consideration of the foe vanquished by her, but was also
looked upon by the adjacent khanates in a far better
light than had been hitherto the case, since, according to Tartar notions, conquest was identical with
murder, plunder and extirpation. Central Asia was
really surprised to find mercy at the hands of the
Christian victor.

Scarcely five years had elapsed when Russia,
anxious to avoid " endless extension," cast her eyes
beyond the Oxus upon the Khan of Khiva, applying
almost literally the meaning of the fable of Æsopus
in accusing the Khiva lamb on the lower course of
the Oxus of troubling her waters in the upper
course. A plea for a *casus belli* was soon unearthed.
The young Khan of Khiva, the son of the very man
upon whom I pronounced a blessing whilst sojourning
in his capital, had vainly endeavoured to apologise
and to give every possible redress. The Russian preparations of war had been ready for a long time, provisions were previously secured on different points,
and General Kauffmann, notoriously fond of theatrical
pageantries, marched through the most perilous route
across bottomless sands from the banks of the
Yaxartes to the Oxus. Strange to say, he chose the
very route upon which I trudged years ago, tormented
and nearly killed by thirst. At the station, *Adam*

Kirligan (the place were men perish) he must have remembered the dervish, for I am told on good authority that he travelled with my book in his hands; and the ominous name of the station would have proved really disastrous to the Russian army if the Uzbegs had had the slightest military foresight, or had been aware of the very rudimentary principles of warfare. The Russians, who marched from three different points upon the khanate, had a very easy task before them. Without fighting a single battle, the whole country on the Lower Oxus was conquered. Russia again showed herself magnanimous by replacing the young Khan upon the paternal throne, after having taken away from him the whole country on the right bank of the Oxus, and imposed upon his neck the burden of a war indemnity which will weigh him down as long as he lives, and cripple even his successors, if any such are to come after him.

Three more years passed, when Russia, anxious to avoid "endless extension," again began to extend the limits of her possessions in the Yaxartes Valley towards the East. In July, 1876, one of the famous Russian embassies of amity was casually (?) present at the Court of Khudayar Khan at Khokand, when suddenly a rebellion broke out, endangering not only the lives of the Russian embassy but also of the allied ruler. No wonder, therefore, that Russia had to take care of the friend in distress. An army was despatched to Khokand, the rebellion was quelled, and, as a natural consequence, the whole khanate incorporated into the dominions of the Czar. The Khokandians, especially one portion of them called the Kiptchaks, did not surrender so easily as their brethren in Bokhara and Khiva. The struggle between the conqueror and the native people was a bloody and protracted one; and the butchery at Namangan, an engagement in which the afterwards famous General Skobeleff won his spurs, surpasses all the accounts hitherto given of Russian cruelty. Similar scenes occurred in Endidjan and other places, until the power of the Kiptchaks, noted for their bravery all over Central Asia, was broken, and "peace," a *pendant* to the famous tableau of Vereshtchagin, "peace at Shipka," prevailed throughout the valleys of Ferghana, enabling the Russian eagle to spread his wings undisturbedly over the whole of Central Asia, beginning from the Caspian Sea in the west to the Issyk Kul in the east, and from Siberia to the Turkoman sands in the south. The conquest of Central Asia was thus literally accomplished, and we shall only dwell on the main reason which has facilitated the success, and enabled Russia to penetrate into the very nest of the hitherto inaccessible Mohammedan fanaticism.

By us in Europe the new feats of Russian arms
were certainly looked upon with great surprise.
Nations vain-glorious of military deeds partly envied
and partly admired the modern successor of Djenghis
and Timur, but it is only ignorance of facts and gross
exaggeration which has led them astray. They had
been accustomed from immemorial times to couple
the names of Tartar, Kalmuk, Kirghis, etc., with all
rudeness, strength, power, and all possibly imaginable
qualities of savage warriors. I had the same opinion
on the subject; but how different was my experience
gathered on the spot, when I discovered in the
roughest-looking Tartar a coward without example,
and found that despite my lame leg I could, armed
with a stick, put to flight five or six men. Of such
a character was the predominant majority of the
enemies Russia had to fight. The whistle of a single
ball was enough to scare away dozens of warlike-
looking Sarts, Tadjiks, and Uzbegs. In reality how
could it be otherwise, considering the difference existing between the arms of the Russian conqueror and
those of the native defenders? Take the gun, for
instance. The Russian is armed with a good modern
rifle, and his gunpowder is of the best, whilst the
poor Tartar has nothing but an old and rusty gun
which rests on a kind of wooden fork. Before attempting to shoot, he is looking out for a level spot

where to put down his wooden fork. He has to place the coarse gunpowder in the pan, then strike fire with the flint to ignite the tinder, and proceeds to tap upon the powder for at least five minutes. The rusty gun bursts, the fork tumbles down, and where the ball has gone to God only knows.

Besides this dissimilarity in arms, we have to consider the utter want of union, which disabled the natives of Central Asia from a vigorous defence of an invading power. Bokhara may well be taken for the leading state in Central Asia; but her influence over the neighbouring khanates was never of such an extent as to rally the Khivans, the Khokandians, and Turkomans around her flag, nor was the Emir himself sufficiently penetrated by the necessity of such assistance. He was proud, haughty, and over self-confident. His conceitedness vied with his stupidity, and when I met him in Samarkand he asked me, amongst other things, whether the Sultan of Turkey could boast of an army as formidable as his own, an army with which he might have conquered China if he were disposed to do so. As to his subjects, I noticed that they had not even the slightest foreboding of the approaching Russian danger, and when alluding to such an eventuality I generally got for an answer: "Hadji, do not speak about it; the soil of Samarkand and Bokhara is so full of the remains of

departed saints and pious Mohammedans that infidels
will die as soon as they set foot upon it." Ludicrous,
childish remarks, which certainly were forgotten when
the armies of Bokhara, Khokand, and Khiva were
defeated; and, strange to say, these very boasting,
overweening men were the first to submit to Russian
rule, and to look upon the new state of things as a
matter long ago decreed by the will of Almighty God.

To sum up briefly, Bokhara, Khiva, and Khokand
fell one after the other. Russia reached the left bank
of the Oxus; she obtained what she had been long
coveting. She now could have rounded off her possessions from Siberia to the very heart of Asia; for in
reaching the Oxus, this old natural frontier between
Iranians and Turanians, she then might have been
satisfied with having brought nearly the whole of
the Tartar race under her sway; the great work of
civilisation which she wrote upon her banners could
have been quietly begun. But the politicians at St.
Petersburg had objects quite different in view.
Humanitarian purposes are only the clever bait
invented to catch the credulous statesmen of Europe.
Russia cherished other far-reaching schemes, in the
furtherance of which she crossed frontiers many a
thousand years old, and, disregarding any eventual
complications, merrily rushed into her adventures on
the left bank of the Oxus.

CHAPTER III.

THE Russian move on the left bank of the Oxus
might have been viewed from the very beginning as
the unmistakable sign of her ulterior designs against
India. In conquering the three khanates of Turkestan, we are disposed to conclude that Russian
politicians made a failure of it, and that they only
subsequently found out that the route leading from
Orenburg towards the Oxus was a very difficult
highway for an army intending to march from the
interior of the mother country towards the Suleiman
range. Judging from the attempt to build a railway from Orenburg to Tashkend, which afterwards
failed, in spite of the exertions of M. Lesseps,
who promised the world to run a train from Calais
to Calcutta, 7,500 miles long, in nine days, we
may assume that the Russians had really over-rated
the possession of the khanates, and found out that
Central Asia, which has ever since charged the
exchequer with a deficit varying of from eight to

ten millions of roubles annually, will never pay, and will always remain a barren acquisition to the State. Well, as far as this burden is concerned, we will not deny the fact that the expenses of a European administration, be it even a Russian one, will never be defrayed by the income. It will always prove an expensive colony—a luxurious acquisition; but Russia had nevertheless to submit to this sacrifice in the interests of her ulterior schemes. She was compelled to secure in her rear a safe position, whilst she had the intention of moving on the main line from the south-west towards the south-east—I mean from southern Russia across the Caucasus, the Caspian, and along the northern border of Persia to the goal of her desire. This was the route originally conceived for the Russian march against India; and the endurance, astuteness, and cleverness with which this line of communication was begun and continued, are really unrivalled in the history of conquering nations.

Our space is too limited to dwell here at length upon the details of this plan, carried on for nearly two centuries. We shall speak rather of that portion which relates to the eastern shore of the Caspian Sea, and state that Russian aggression dates as far back as 1825, when the afterwards famous Muravieff started on his mission to Khiva from Krasnovodsk, in order to explore the desert and to bring home information

about this little or scarcely known tract of country.
Immediately after him followed in 1835 Karelin, who
investigated the shore from the Gurgan river as far as
Krasnovodsk, and since that time scarcely a year has
elapsed without some Russian officers, under the guise
of the famous Russian scientific expeditions, visiting
this shore to continue the explorations. The result of
it was that whilst the rest of Europe remained in utter
ignorance about the people and the country on the
eastern shore of the Caspian, Russia was pretty well
informed as to the geographical position of that country,
as well as to the mutual relations of the Turkoman
inhabitants. The picture drawn by Galkin may well
be defective, but it is the first reliable report, and I
do not exaggerate when I state that since the occupation of Ashurada Russians were by no means
strangers amongst the Yomuts and Goklans. Having
duly reconnoitered the country, the proper move
against the Turkomans began only after the subjugation of the three khanates, and particularly after the
horrible massacre of the Turkomans subject to Khiva
in 1873. The bloody affair of Kizil-Takir, in which
nearly 10,000 Turkoman Yomuts lost their lives,
chilled the blood of their brethren on the south of
the Balkans. The Russian position at Tchekishlar
was easily secured, and in fact no serious fight took
place during the whole time that the Russians had

entered the country of the Yomuts, until the period
when they came into contact with the next Turkoman
tribes, namely, the Tekkes, who inhabit the country
eastward of the Yomuts, and who were at all times
noted for their strength, wealth, and courage. At
the hands of the Tekke-Turkomans, particularly of
the Akhal section of them, the Russian army experienced more than one disagreeable surprise for
imagining they had before them opponents like the
Uzbegs, Sarts, and Tadjiks of the three khanates, or
Turkomans of the caste of Yomuts. They awoke to
the consciousness of having to deal with a hardy race,
ready to fight and to defend their homes, in spite of
the inferiority of their arms.

The history of the defeats of Lomakin, of the unsuccessful attack of Lazareff, and of the heavy cost in
blood and money incurred by the various Russian expeditions, is too fresh in memory to be recalled here
again. Thanks to the useful and well-known publications of Charles Marvin, we may forego enumerating
the details of the siege and capture of Geok-Tepe by
Skobeleff in 1880. Suffice it to say, that courageous
and heroic as was the defence of the besieged Turkomans, who fought under the lead of Makhdum-Kuli
and Tekme Serdar, their two chieftains, the hardships
and privations the Russians had to endure, and the
extraordinary cool blood and doggedness they exhibited

at that time, was in keeping with it.   Out of 40,000
Turkomans, huddled up in the fortress of Geok-Tepe,
6,500 bodies were found inside the fortress, 8,000
fugitives were slaughtered, many hundreds of women
and children were killed, so that nearly half of the
garrison perished.   "During the actual assault and
in the subsequent pursuit, the infantry engaged fired
273,804 rounds, the cavalry 12,500, and the artillery 5,864 rounds ; 224 military rockets were also
expended " (Marvin).   With this successful stroke
against the Akhal-Tekke Turkomans, Russia had
almost entirely broken the strength and power of the
hitherto mostly dreaded nomads of Central Asia.
Thanks to the effect of modern arms and to her
drilled army, she accomplished a feat neither Djenghis
Khan nor Timur, or any of the Asiatic conquerors
could boast of.

The Turkomans, numbering about a million of
souls, justly enjoyed in antiquity, and do still at present, the fame of being the best horsemen and the
most valiant warriors all over Asia.   Having lived
amongst them in the very height of their independence, and having had opportunity to witness their
daily life and to study their character, I am bound to
fully subscribe to the above quoted estimate of their
reputation.   "Allah first, then our horse and arms,
and then in the third place our family and relations,"

is a common saying amongst them, and the care the Turkoman bestows upon his horse and upon his arms is far superior to the tenderness he is in the habit of showing to his wife and children. A proverb amongst them says, "If you see a party attacking the house of your father and mother, join them in the plunder and robbery;" and indeed, so utterly boundless is their desire for forays, battles, and daring adventures, that for want of a better opportunity they fall upon each other, even for the sake of a very trifling matter. The fatigue and hardship which these fellows can endure is most wonderful; not less their pluck and contempt of death, and albeit they say that, "Try twice, and if you do not succeed turn back the third time;" it very rarely occurs that the double attack of a Turkoman should fail to obtain the object in view. As to the dread they used to spread among the neighbouring nations, I will only quote one instance, of which I myself was an eye-witness. Having been asked one day to bestow my blessing upon a party ready for a foray, I took the rather curious fancy to join the fellows, and to be present at one of their engagements. Crossing the Gurgan, we entered the Persian terri- tory; I found myself side by side with the Serdar— *i.e.*, leading man. He spied with his eagle eyes into the environs around him, and his appearance alone was sufficient to put a travelling company of Persians,

consisting of about forty men, to a disgraceful flight.
No wonder that these fellows became the dread and
terror, not only of all Persia, into which they penetrated in small bands from a hundred to a hundred
and fifty miles into the interior, but also to the rest
of Central Asia, particularly to Bokhara, Khiva, and
to the very walls of Maimene. "May you fall into
the hands of the Turkoman," was the most bitter
curse; and the saying, "Khouf-i-Turkmen"—*i.e.*, fear
of the Turkoman, was able to chill the blood even of
the bravest of Asiatics, with the exception of the
Afghans, who frequently had proved an unequal
match for them.

Such was the people vanquished by Skobeleff at
Geok-Tepe, such the enemy which Russia crushed
in the north of Persia; and the reader may easily
imagine how these feats of arms had raised the consideration of Russia in the eyes of all the Asiatics.
First of all came admiration of the military strength
and valour of the White Padishah on the banks of the
Neva, who had surpassed in glory and greatness even
the names of Djenghis, Timur, and Nadir. No less
deep was the impression of gratitude wrought in the
feelings of the Persians by the Russian success in the
steppes of the Turkomans. Exposed for centuries to
the irruptions of these reckless nomads, the peaceful
and industrious inhabitants of Iran had vainly looked

for assistance to their king and government; the round tower of shelter erected on their fields could afford but a temporary refuge, and the final redemption from the inveterate enemy and terrible plague came only from the hand of a Christian ruler, from Russia, which now was called the real redeemer of half of Persia. It will remain an ever deplorable fact, that England, by whose civilising work so very many Asiatics have been benefited hitherto, did not try to anticipate her rival in this great work, considering that she could have done it more easily and much better. As to Persia, rotten to the very core, the ministers of the Shah, when asked about their feelings for the services rendered by the Russians, impudently remarked, "We did not invite the Muscovites to deliver us from the Turkomans, nor do we feel particularly grateful to them for having done so."

The feeling of the people, however, was widely different. Along the whole route through Khorassan, beginning from Shahrud, to Meshed and Sarakhs, but more particularly in the districts adjoining the newly acquired Russian territory, namely in Kabushan, Budjnurd, and Deregöz, people are now most anxious to exhibit their sympathies with the northern conqueror. Russian dresses are becoming the fashion of the day, Russian drinks get more and more into favour, every man of note strives to learn the Russian language,

D

and there is no exaggeration in saying that Russia has already morally conquered the northern slopes of the Kubbet Mountains to such an extent, that the physical conquest is only a question of time.

The next benefit Russia will derive from the subjugation of the Akhal-Tekke Turkomans, will be found in the strategical as well as commercial position she gained through her standing on the southern slopes of the Kubbet Mountains, known in antiquity as the country of the Parthians. Excepting the embouchures of the Gurgan, the eastern shore of the Caspian Sea is, as far as Kizil-Arvat, nothing but a dreary desert, a sterile and an arid country. Cultivation, owing to irrigation carried from the mountain, begins only at the last-named place. But the more we advance eastward the richer becomes the soil, the more plentiful is the water in the irrigating canals, and the more varied and luxuriant are the products. In fact, up to the beginning of the thirteenth century, this country was noted for its fertility and for its centres of culture. In antiquity, the great commercial road leading from the interior of Asia to the west, has passed the southern slopes of the Kubbet Mountain to the Caspian, and in spite of having been laid waste by the irruption of the Mongols, the places of Kahka and Mehne, Abiverd, and some others, enjoyed a fair amount of reputation up to the end of the seventeenth century. Nothing, therefore, is easier to surmise than that Russia, being in the undisputed possession of that rich country, will do all in her power to revive the bygone period of culture. The country could be much more quickly colonised and peopled than any of her more recent acquisitions in Turkestan. Russia is prompted to hasten the process of colonisation here, in order to get a firm footing on the eastern shore of the Caspian Sea, on the very spot which is calculated to become the second link of connection in her great chain of communication, running from the interior of Russia over the Black Sea, the Caucasus, and the Caspian, to the outskirts of the Paropamisus. It was in full recognition of this important fact that the Caucasus was bridged over by rail from Batoum to Baku, at the cost of £9,000,000 ; and considering the extraordinary increase of private and governmental ships on the Caspian during the last twenty years, it was but natural that the Russian government did not shun the expense, but began, simultaneously with the conquest of Turkomania, the construction of the Trans-caspian railway, which until quite recently, starting from Mikhailofsk on the Balkan Bay, stretched over 144 miles to Kizil-Arvat, involving a cost of £648,000.

The heavy blow inflicted, Russia's first care was to pacify the country, and to show to the Turkomans that the Czar was not only able to strike hard, but that he also possessed the power to heal the wounds, to show mercy, and to become a kind-hearted father of his subjects. Skobeleff, the originator of the massacre, and the dreaded exterminator of the Turkomans, was recalled from the scene of his bloody action and replaced by General Röhrberg, a Germano-Russian officer noted for his administrative faculties, and evidently the best man to represent the benignant rays of the sun after the frightful storm which had swept over the Akhal country. He began by alluring the large masses of fugitives which were dispersed in every direction of the less accessible sands in the north of the Karakum, invited them to re-occupy their former places, petted and encouraged them to go on with their usual work, promising, and giving too, all kinds of assistance; they were only asked to give up the arms they had concealed, and to keep quiet under the new order of things which awaited them. The returning Akhal-Tekke Turkomans presented the most pitiful aspect of dreary desolation and bewilderment; the greater portion of their property was lost and scattered; more than half of their cattle had perished in the desert. The haggard-looking and terror-stricken nomads, happy to save the last resources of existence, were certainly the best material out of which the first nucleus of

Russian peaceful subjects in the desert could be formed.

The Government did all in its power to attract the sympathies of these poor wretches, but the Muscovite soldiery could not be restrained from pillaging to the last these half-naked inhabitants of the formerly flourishing Akhal country. Carpets, rugs, trinkets, jewellery, particularly arms inlaid with gold and silver, rich harnesses and saddles, went in loads beyond the Caspian and the Caucasus to Russia; and so great was the booty carried away from the desert, and sold in the various Russian towns, that part of it even reached Hungary, and the writer of these lines had an opportunity of buying in Buda-Pesth carpets, embroideries, and jewellery, the former property of Turkoman women. The merchant who offered these wares for sale, a Caucasian, who took part in the war, an eye-witness of the Russian depredations, remarked boastfully—" Sir, we have paid back to those rascals the many hundred years' cruelties and robberies; a part of them we have sent to hell; and the remaining part we have left *lukht-i-pukht* (naked and wretched), giving them full time and opportunity to ruminate over the greatness of the white Czar, who is of quite a different cast from the cowardly Kadjar in Teheran." And indeed the *lukht-i-pukht* Turkomans submitted in the full sense of the word, and had to begin a life to which certainly they had not been accustomed hitherto. The evil most sensibly felt was the exceedingly thinned ranks of the male population, and I hear from quite recent travellers that polygamy, hitherto scarcely known amongst Turkomans, has become an imperative necessity, and that, in order to provide for widows and girls matrimonially inclined, one Turkoman has to take frequently from six to eight wives, a burden exceeding his means of subsistence; poverty being the natural consequence of this anomaly.

CHAPTER IV.

As to the Russians, they chose Ashkabad, a word literally meaning *the abode of love*, for the new centre of administration. It became the gathering place of the leading officers as well as of the mercantile world, following in the track of the invading army. The merchants, mostly Caucasians, Mohammedans and Christian Armenians, able to converse with the Turkomans—for the Turkish spoken by the Turkomans differs but slightly from the dialect spoken in the Caucasus—were decidedly the best means of communication between the natives and the foreign conqueror. They could penetrate unmolested even to the far outlying parts of the Akhal country, for the Turkoman, once vanquished and sincerely submitting, would not touch any of the solitary travellers. These merchants enlarged upon the greatness and might of the Russians, spoke of the charity of the Czar, and bridged over smoothly and quietly the wide gulf existing but a short time ago between the dreaded

Russ and the Turkoman. As to commercial affairs, they were in the beginning unimportant, and most of the customers came from the ranks of the Russian army; but gradually the Turkomans, too, began to purchase sundry articles, and in particular took very quickly to the shops of the spirit-vendors, whose trade soon became most flourishing. In the course of two years six different whisky distilleries were opened in Ashkabad and the adjacent country; and so rapid was the spread of European civilisation *à la Russe*, that even playing-cards, known formerly under the name of "the koran of the Muscovites," had found their way to the tent of the simple Turkoman.

Of other phases of the new era of civilisation I will not speak: suffice to mention that the Turkomans very soon delighted in wearing big brass medals on their breasts and adorning their shoulders with epaulettes, and only the female population and the older people were anxious to retain their ancient national character, and avoid any closer intercourse with the foreign conqueror. Kismet, *i.e.*, fate, or properly speaking, an absolute reliance upon the decrees of the Almighty, proved anew its efficacy; and all the more natural was this effect with the Turkomans, whose national bard, called Makhdum-Kuli, predicted nearly a hundred years ago the events which had just now come into fulfilment.

In a poem entitled "The End of the World," the
Turkoman poet relates, in his plain but impressive
language, how the towns and countries (of course
within the sphere of his geographical information)
will perish, how the various nations will disappear off
the face of the earth, and at the end of his poem he
says :

> "It is the *Russ* who will engulf the Moslem world,
> Whilst the Russ will be swallowed by the Anti-Christ."

But let us return to Ashkabad. This place,
made the centre of the Russian administration, as
well as of the new cultural and commercial movement, very soon attracted not only those Turkomans
who were already under the sway of the Russians,
but also such members of that community as still
enjoyed their independence—I mean to say Turkomans from Merv, from the Tedjend oasis, nay, even
from the Salor and Sarik tribes, who, prompted
partly by curiosity, partly by trading purposes, re-
sorted to this place in order to see the new master
of the country. I can fully imagine the surprise
of these Turkomans upon finding themselves safe
in the very midst of the dreaded conquerors; for
according to their own notions of the mutual relations between belligerents, the only chance that could
have awaited a foreigner would have been death or

slavery. I say the surprise must have been extraordinary; it discarded all fear, nay, turned to a certain extent into sympathy for the new cause.

It was Merv, in particular, that sent a large contingent of trading and sight-seeing guests to Ashkabad! Merv, the head-quarters of the yet independent and larger portion of the Tekke Turkomans; for it must be borne in mind that whilst the number of the Akhal-Tekke Turkomans is computed to be about 150,000 souls, that of the Merv-Tekkes is estimated at 250,000. I spoke about sight-seers from Merv, but I must add at the same time, that the Russians were no less anxious to get a peep at Merv, and to see the "Queen of the World," this being the pompous title given to the miserable heap of ruins by Oriental writers. In antiquity, or properly speaking during the pre-Mongolian era, Merv really was a great centre of culture and trade in this outlying part of Persia; and old Arab geographers speak of hundreds of gates, of hundreds of mosques, of thousands of palaces, baths, of miles of bazaars, of spacious caravansaries, etc., for which Merv was famous. Abstracting the poetical flavour of Oriental geographers, we may assume that Merv had really been a large town in bygone times; for, situated on the banks of the Murghab river, and richly watered, it was the best halting place for caravans trading

between Bokhara and Persia. But its splendour,
as I said before, has long since passed away; the
army of Djenghis turned it into a heap of ruins; and
all later efforts to rebuild it have proved hopeless and
futile.

Yet Russia, always alive to her interests, very well
knew what Merv was worth. Soon after having
settled at Ashkabad, she coveted it, for it was in
her line of policy, and only to avoid the charge
of greediness she thought it advisable to adopt
quiet measures and to feign moderation. In the
beginning the rumour was propagated that Merv,
having been in olden times an integral part of the
khanate of Khiva, which had been really the case,
this last stronghold of the Turkomans would be handed
over to the Khan of Khiva; and it was even added
that the Turkomans themselves were longing after
their former state of suzerainty to the khanate on the
lower course of the Oxus. I read this news in a Persian paper, and was highly amused at the ingenious idea
the Russians entertained, of using the Khan of Khiva
as a catspaw in the troublesome affair of Merv.
Soon afterwards this rumour turned out to be untrue.
Röhrberg was removed on grounds which have remained unknown to us, and General Komaroff took
his place; the latter a genuine Russian of unadulterated Muscovite extraction, a man certainly fitter

for the task of throwing out the line and hook in the dark waters of Turkoman affairs than the aforesaid German officer, who, in spite of his long services to the Czar, must have retained too much of European honesty to work successfully in the Asiatic gangway of plots and intrigues.

To us, the lookers on from a distance, the relations between Ashkabad and Merv were utterly unknown, and we were prepared for a solid resistance on the part of the Mervians. The Russian authorities at Ashkabad, however, had a better insight into that matter. They saw the continually increasing number of Mervians coming to Ashkabad for shopping, and the idea naturally occurred to them to persuade these people that, if they liked, the Russian merchants themselves would come to Merv, and bring with them the goods they had a hankering after. Whether the Turkomans of Merv agreed to that act of politeness we do not decidedly know; but it is a fact that a caravan was soon got ready, and started in February, 1882, for Merv, not, however, before Fazil Beg, an Uzbeg of Khiva, Russianised in consequence of his repeated journeys to Russia, had been sent to explore the place, and to secure protection for the caravan.

Alikhanoff, known by his family name Avarski, which means an Avar, a tribe of the Daghestan, was at the head of this caravan. He belonged to that class of Russian officers who, without forsaking their religion, become thoroughly Russianised, partly through the education they get and partly through long intercourse with their fellow-officers. By placing an " off," which corresponds with the English " son," at the end of their names, they adopt the Russian nationality officially; and combining, as they do, a smattering of European education with Asiatic astuteness, they generally turn out very clever men, and have often rendered essential services to the Russian State. Such Russianised Tartars were, amongst others, Velikhanoff, the famous traveller in Kashgar, the Naziroffs, Tahiroffs, Muratoffs, etc., and such is the Russianised Kalmukian Dondukoff Korsakoff, who, in spite of parading his French eloquence, had a Kalmukian grandfather, Donduk Korsak.

As to the biography of Alikhanoff, whose fame has recently spread all over the western world, I would refer the reader to Charles Marvin's "The Russians at the Gates of Herat," a cleverly written book, full of information gathered from Russian sources. Suffice it to say that Alikhanoff went in the disguise of a trader, and, acting as the interpreter and clerk to the Russian merchant Kosikh, he succeeded in entering Merv, and was, together with his Russian colleagues, pretty well received by Makhdum-Kuli Khan, the very Turkoman chieftain who led the defence of

Geok-Tepe, and escaping, together with Teknic Serdar, has since, by dint of Russian gifts, entirely changed his mind by becoming a secret friend of his former deadly enemy. As to the wares the so-called Russian traders brought with them, they must have been disposed of in a way not dissimilar to that used nearly forty years ago by Conolly on his journey across the country of the Yomuts; with this only difference, that whilst the British officer tried to buy his way through plundering nomads, the Russian traders in disguise aimed at, and succeeded, in purchasing a place of strategical and commercial importance, with the sole object of hoodwinking Europe and more particularly England.

After having remained a fortnight in Merv, the pseudo-merchants returned safely to Ashkabad, taking with them the conviction that Merv would not have to be bought with torrents of blood like Geok-Tepe, and that it wanted only some time and patience to make the half-ripe apple drop into the lap of the Russian Emperor. Among the acquisitions made by Alikhanoff, belongs the promise of Makhdum-Kuli Khan to be present at the coronation of the Emperor Alexander II. at Moscow, where his presence greatly raised the splendour of Oriental pageantry, affording besides ample opportunity to the wild nomad to relate wonders on his return among his countrymen

of the pomp and the greatness of the White Padishah
on the Neva. The splendour of the festivities he
saw dazzled his eyes and I can imagine how his accounts, assisted by his Oriental fancy, must have
roused his listeners to wonder and amazement

Whilst these incidents were going on, General
Komaroff also stretched out a feeler towards the
south-east of the Turkoman country, by sending
Col. Muratoff from Ashkabad to the Tedjend oasis,
a distance of about 130 miles, partly in order to
prepare the march around the north-eastern frontiers
of Persia, partly, too, to serve as an outpost against
Merv, ninety miles distant, with the view that,
should the amicable transactions fail, the Cossacks
might hurry to put an emphasis upon the Russian
declaration of love. As matters turned out afterwards, this precaution was justified. In the beginning of 1884 events in Merv were ripe for the swoop.
Alikhanoff appeared, accompanied only by a few horsemen and the hero of Geok-Tepe, at Merv, and
read before a public meeting the letter of General
Komaroff he had brought with him, in which the
people of Merv were summoned to submit to the
rule of Russia. On his alluding to his being able to
emphasise his summons with the Cossacks at the
Tedjend oasis, the principal Aksakals, or "Grey-
beards," instantaneously set their seal to that ominous

document. Alikhanoff turned to Ashkabad, bringing with him four chiefs and twenty-four notables, who took the oath of allegiance on the 6th of February, 1884, in General Komaroff's drawing-room. M. Henri Moser, a Swiss traveller, who happened to be present at that time at Ashkabad, gave me some interesting details about the hurry and secrecy with which this act was accomplished.

The Turkoman elders, in order to please their new masters, had brought amongst sundry presents a few Persian slaves of both sexes, presents in exchange for which they got sums of money, robes of honour, and arms of European construction. As to these elders, the comedy of voluntary submission was at an end; but not as to those other Turkomans remaining at Merv, whose allegiance had not yet been bought over, and who would have shown strong resistance to the so-called "voluntary submission" if they had been forewarned and in time prepared for an effective resistance. As things stood, the sufficiently numerous anti-Russian party was taken as it were by surprise; they succeeded only in firing a few shots in the form of a protest, and, although several thousands of them attacked the Russians under the lead of Kadjar Khan, they were at once repulsed and routed. Kadjar Khan took refuge in Afghan territory; his adherents tacitly submitted; and the Russian army

occupied, on the 16th of March, the Kalai-Khurshid
Khan, erroneously called in Europe Koshut Khan, in
one corner of which the Russians have since erected a
fort called Nikolayeffsk.

Thus fell Merv, the "Queen of the World"—in
a European prosaic translation, a heap of ruins—into
the hands of Russia. Alikhanoff was raised to the
rank of a major; Makhdum-Kuli Khan was rewarded by being appointed as the head of the Tedjend oasis ; Komaroff got the order of the White
Eagle, and was made Governor-General of Transcaspia. Other participators were likewise distinguished, and in order to cap the climax, Dondukoff
Korsakoff, the Governor-General of the Caucasus, the
man who denounced the Treaty of Berlin as a piece of
music *à la Offenbach*, very soon afterwards appeared
in Merv to proclaim to the "voluntarily submitting"
Turkomans the great joy and satisfaction the White
Padishah at the Neva had evinced at this spon-
taneous act of his beloved Turkoman children.
Evidently knowing the gluttonous and greedy character of these new members of the large Russian
family, the ex-Kalmuk Dondukoff was also the bearer
of a large quantity of brandy, of robes of honour, etc.,
which were distributed amongst the leading Turkomans. The Court of St. Petersburg even took an
active part in the so-called "voluntary submission"

E

of the Mervians, for we read in the correspondence of a Russian officer, published in the *Turkestan Gazette* of May, 1885, that the Empress sent a richly embroidered dress, said to be her own needlework, to the widow of the late Nurverdi Khan, named Gul-Djemal, *i.e.*, "Beauty of the Rose," a lady of great influence amongst the Mervians, who had no little share in that "voluntary submission."

Summing up what we said in reference to the Russian acquisition of Merv, we may well conclude with the remark that it was a clever stroke on the part of the Cabinet of St. Petersburg to secure this outlying post of the Turkoman country, and that for the following reasons :—

1. By the annexation of Merv, and by subduing the whole Tekke tribe, Russia has made nearly the whole Turkoman nation her subjects. The Turkoman possessions could now be rounded off into one compact body, and no further apprehension had to be entertained concerning the enmity of the people.

2. The situation of Merv, midway between Bokhara and Persia, offered the best means of communication between the newly laid down railway on the eastern shore of the Caspian Sea, and the trading *route* between the Zerefshan and eastern Persia. The news which has reached us lately referring to

the connection of a railroad from Bokhara to Merv, and to Sarakhs, must be looked upon as a natural consequence of this central position. It had been from immemorial times a highway between the khanates and Persia; and Russia having done away with the Turkoman nuisance, is almost sure to drain off the whole of the Central Asian trade to this newly-planned channel.

3. By rendering innocuous any future hostile movements of the Tekke-Turkomans in Merv, Russia has removed any obstacle possibly arising on her flanks at a time when she might intend to move on her main line of communication from Sarakhs towards Herat; and by doing so, she has successfully imitated all the Asiatic conquerors who burst forth from Central Asia with the open intention to attack and conquer India. Just as Alexander the Great secured the old Marghiana (Merv) before entering the Afghanistan of to-day, in the same way we find the army of Djenghis occupying and destroying Merv before it entered Herat. The same thing was done by Timur, the Uzbeg Sheibani Khan, and Nadir Shah. It was therefore quite in accordance with the principles of strategy, that Alexander III. possessed himself of Merv to further his ulterior plans upon India. Similar to these views of mine are the opinions of many other contemporary English

E 2

writers on that subject, and for the sake of endorsement I shall quote the following authorities :—

General Sir Edward Hamley, undoubtedly one of the greatest living authorities on military topics, said amongst other things, "The one advantage of the possession (of Merv) is that the caravan route passing Bokhara to Meshed and the interior, and that from India by Herat to Central Asia, lie through Merv. But that it was once a centre of great prosperity, is proved by the fact that the remains of four great cities exist there, the inhabitants of the last of which were driven out by the semi-barbarians about a century ago. Under Russian rule that prosperity will revive, the lands will once more teem with the crops to which nothing is wanting but good husbandry, and, when once again become populous and fertile, it will form a secondary base against the Afghan frontier. In the meantime it closes the gap aforesaid, and as soon as Russia lays down her frontier line, the whole of that vast empire, from the Baltic to the Danube, thence along the Black Sea, across the Caucasus to the Caspian, along the Persian frontier to Merv and Turkestan, and so on to Siberia, will lie in a ring fence. This is the power which is now separated from a frontier which, presumably, we cannot allow her to overstep, by a border land which is a barrier in no sense, and which I will endeavour briefly to describe."

Colonel Valentine Baker wrote on his return from the Perso-Turkoman frontier in 1873 : " Merv, with its water communication nearly complete, lies only 240 miles from Herat, to which place it is the key.   There can be no doubt that Merv is the natural outwork of Herat, with the advantage of water supply all the way between the two cities. Strategically, the Russian occupation of Merv would be, so to say, the formation of a lodgment on the glacis of Herat.   It would place Herat completely at her mercy."

Sir Charles Macgregor wrote in 1875 : " There is no doubt in my mind that the real danger lies in our permitting the Russians to concentrate unopposed at Merv, which is quite within *coup de main* distance of Herat ; and it is in this fact that the value of Merv to the Russians lies.   Once place Herat beyond the possibility of a *coup de main*, and I cannot imagine the astute statesmen of Russia persisting in the occupation of an isolated spot in the desert, the maintenance of which must cost a great deal."

Finally, we may quote the words of ⹁Charles Marvin, written in February, 1884 : " The conquest of Merv is something more than the annexation of a sand-desert oasis.   It means the complete junction of the military forces of the Caucasus and Turkestan. It means, with the annexation of Akhal, the absorption of 100,000 of the best irregular cavalry in the world, at a week's march from the city of Herat. It means the meeting, for the first time, of the Cossack and the Afghan. It means the complete enclosure of Khiva within the Russian Empire, and the reduction of Bokhara from the independent position of a border state to the dependence of an incorporated province. It means the enclosure of more than 200,000 square miles of territory, and the addition to the Russian Empire of a region as large as France. It means the completion of the conquest of the Central Asian deserts, and the commencement of the annexation of the great fertile mountain region of Persia and Afghanistan. It means the deliberate occupation of a strategical point, fraught with political entanglements of such a widespread nature that, whether Russia desire it or not, she will be inevitably led, unless forestalled or checked by England, to Meshed, to Herat, to Balkh, and to Kabul. And she will not remain there. She will continue her swift advance until she triumphantly lays down her Cossack border alongside the Sepoy line of India."

I could easily add other statements by English and foreign authorities on that subject, but I suppose I have succeeded in proving that Merv, although actually a heap of ruins, haunted by reckless robbers and lawless bands, is by no means that worthless piece of sand described by optimistic politicians; for if the sand be removed there may be found a precious jewel of military and commercial importance beneath the arid crust.

CHAPTER V.

WE have followed hitherto the history of Russian
conquests from Tashkend to Merv. We have given
a succinct account of the varied events, without inter-
rupting our relation by a side glance upon the attitude which the partly mediate, partly immediate,
neighbours have maintained during the whole course
of Russian encroachment. We shall now turn to
this question, and begin by showing the views exhibited in England in the face of these emergencies.
In England, where the liveliest interest ought to
have prevailed, nevertheless, we are sorry to remark that criminal indifference, coupled with utter
want of courage and lack of due appreciation of the
question, have marked the whole long process of her
diplomatic relations with Russia, as well as of the
defensive steps taken in that direction.

In the beginning, when the black cloud loomed
up in the north, there was a sufficient amount of

anxiety; nay, even too much of it was shown concerning the approaching danger of Russian aggression. But, as is usually the case with a danger of
long standing, the fire gradually slackened until it
came quite recently to a final extinction, wrapping
the vital interests of Great Britain in that ominous
darkness in which she is now actually groping.

When, in the beginning of the present century,
Napoleon I. united with Russia, and the plan of
crippling England through an attack on India first
appeared, the Anglo-Indian statesmen of that day
had shown sufficient vigour in grasping the importance of the situation. The building of the English
rule in India rested on a ricketty base, and the danger
was serious, considering the intentions of the Emperor,
Paul I., made afterwards public through his auto-
graph letters directed to Prince Orloff, the chief of
the Cossacks (January 12, 1801): "The English are
preparing to make an attack with their fleet and
army against me and my allies, the Swedes and
Danes. We must attack them ourselves, and that at
a spot where the blow should be felt most and be
least expected. From Orenburg to India there is but
three months' (?) marching, and from us to Orenburg
one month—total, four months. I place this expedition in your hands and those of your troops. This
enterprise may procure glory for all of you, may

obtain wealth for us, and open a new outlet for the disposal of our merchandise, thus striking at the enemy's heart." And further on :—" We must liberate the natives (subject to England) ; as to the soil it must be placed in the same dependence upon Russia in which it now is as to England, we must take the entire commerce into our hands." In the letter of January 13, 1801, we read :—" I send you a new map of India, which enters quite into details. On your march make sure of Bokhara for Russia, in order that the Chinese may not get hold of it." (W. Danewsky, " La Russie et L'Angleterre dans L'Asie Centrale." London, 1881 ; p. 25).

To this kind of schemes, boldly conceived but premature for execution, the mission entrusted to Sir John Malcolm was a due and appropriate answer. This highly talented English statesman easily succeeded in frustrating the effect of the French missions under Gardanne and Joubert, for the appearance of Malcolm, furnished with rich means by the Indian Government, was quite sufficient to baffle the efforts of French and Russian diplomacy. What Malcolm began was valiantly continued by Sir Gore Ouseley, and other subsequent British ministers at the Court of Teheran. Persia took nicely to the lesson of European civilisation; the Crown Prince of Persia had a particular fancy for the English language, and the British

.officers employed to drill the Persian army in the European style had answered beyond all expectation. For a time the tide of Persian sympathies for England ran very high, and naturally became the envy of Russia. A quarrel was soon pitched upon, which resulted in the Perso-Russian war, the disastrous end of which was the treaty of Turkman-chai, by which the Caspian Sea was turned into a Russian lake, and Persia was taught the lesson that English assurances in times of anxiety were of no great value in times of distress. No wonder, therefore, that the Shah's sympathies turned at once towards Russia, and English influence from that time began rapidly to go downwards. As men in their proper places are apt to work wonders, we must not be astonished that Sir Henry Rawlinson succeeded during the time of his mission to Persia in restoring the lost *prestige* of England in Teheran to its former place. Being, however, insufficiently supported by the Ministry on the Thames, his ability came to nought, and he very soon returned to Europe.

Since that time England's position in Persia has always been a secondary one, compared with the almighty and ubiquitous influence of Russia. There was no lack of gifted and zealous English ambassadors; but what use is there in the official zeal of single individuals, if the leading statesmen of the

home Government are unable or unwilling to second
the aspirations of their representatives abroad. Persia
was said to have become once and for ever unworthy
of the care bestowed on her, and, by giving up every
hope of winning her over to Western civilisation, she
was left alone, *i.e.*, in the fatal embraces of her
northern wooer.

Russia, finding her way unchecked in this part of
the Asiatic world, very soon set to work to utilise
the favourable opportunity offered to her, by med-
dling with Afghanistan through Persia, as we had
occasion to allude to in our previous pages. She thus
became the real cause of the first Anglo-Afghan war;
for, whatever may have been the reasons of the dispute between Dost Mohammed Khan and Lord
Auckland, the former certainly would not have ventured to enter publicly upon hostilities with Great
Britain, whose power and greatness he knew so well,
if Russia, by her secret and public missions, had not
fomented his hatred and encouraged the otherwise
cautious ruler of Afghanistan to measure swords with
England. During this first Anglo-Afghan war the
English policy of vigilance against Russia had
reached its climax. As I previously remarked, it
went even beyond the proper limits; for the Russian
outposts stood at that time very, very far from any
point that might have been styled the gate of India.

But, alas ! it is with States as it is with individuals
in the ordinary concerns of life.   Extraordinarily
vigorous actions are almost inevitably followed by re-
action ; the excessive English vigilance inaugurated by
the somewhat rash policy of Lord Auckland gradually
turned into carelessness and indifference, from the
time following the conclusion of the disastrous first
Afghan campaign.   The bleaching bones of the English soldiers left beyond the Kheiber Pass, the unexampled treachery, cruelty, and savageness of the
Afghan opponent, seem to have left an indelible
impression on the minds of the English.   Add to
this the accounts of the horrible murder of Stoddart
and Conolly in Bokhara, and you will understand
pretty well the detestation and scorn the English
manifested of all matters connected with Afghan and
Central Asia in general.   Oh yes! we can understand, but not justify this aversion; for any other
European 'power better qualified to deal with the
Asiatics than the English are, would certainly have
avoided the catastrophes connected with this campaign, and even if visited by misfortune, would not
allow herself to be scared away altogether.   Look at
Russia.   In spite of defeats by the score, she did not
relax in her arduous work in the Caucasus until the
most inaccessible gorges of rocks were cleared, and
her victorious banner was made to float over all the

Caucasus. Similar proofs of her perseverance she gave in her fights against the Turkomans, when, three times repulsed with severe wounds she again drew the sword, and did not give in until the enemy was crushed and the Akhal-Tekkes were lying at her feet. Of the reasons of this yielding spirit of the English we shall speak hereafter: suffice to say here, that the epoch of English indifference concerning Russia's dealings in Central Asia dates from this period. Such is the official tone that prevailed, with slight interruptions since that time, in Downing Street as well as on the Hoogly; and if the individual views of certain ministers and leading statesmen occasionally proved an exception to this rule, the exception and the isolated facts proceeding from it are not sufficient in themselves to alter the whole line of premeditated policy.

Thus, many persons will find it rather surprising that Lord Palmerston could have feigned indifference to the Russian conquest of Tashkend, considering his views expressed as follows in a letter written to Lord Clarendon, July 31, 1851:—"The policy and practice of the Russian Government has always been to push forward its encroachments as fast and as far as the apathy or want of firmness of other Governments would allow it to go, but always to stop and retire when it was met with decided resistance, and then to wait for the next favourable opportunity to make another spring on its intended victim. In furtherance of this policy, the Russian policy has always had two strings to its bow— moderate language and disinterested professions at St. Petersburg and at London; active aggression by its agents on the scene of operations. If the aggressions succeed locally, the St. Petersburg Government adopts them as a *fait accompli* which it did not intend, but cannot in honour recede from. If the local agents fail, they are disavowed and recalled, and the language previously held is appealed to as a proof that the agents have overstepped their instructions. . This was exemplified in the treaty of Unkiar-Skelessi, and in the exploits of Simonitch and Vitkovitch in Persia. Orloff succeeded in extorting the treaty of Unkiar-Skelessi from the Turks, and it was represented as a sudden thought, suggested by the circumstances of the time and place, and not the result of any previous instructions; but, having been done, it could not be undone. On the other hand, Simonitch and Vitkovitch failed in getting possession of Herat, in consequence of our vigorous measures of resistance; and as they had failed they were disavowed and recalled, and the language previously held at St. Petersburg was appealed to as a proof of the sincerity of the disavowal, although no human being with two ideas in his head could for a moment doubt that they had acted under specific instructions."

It is, therefore, beyond every doubt that in spite of outspoken anti-Russian feelings, and notwithstanding the Crimean war, a costly and quite objectless undertaking, the attitude of British statesmen in relation to Russian encroachments in Central Asia has had, from the first, that mark of leniency, indecision, and irresolution which has unfortunately prevailed up to the present time. Here and there we may have noticed an effervescence, a dubious rushing into action; but very soon abating, and always lame and without results in the end. Thus we find that during the whole conquest, from Tashkend to Bokhara, scarcely a voice was raised against advancing Russia. The public mind of England was swayed by her humanitarian swindling; and whenever the writer of these lines demonstrated the danger which was sure to arise out of the Russian advance to India, he was mostly pooh-poohed by the leading organs of both parties, nay, even rebuked for attempting to check the benignant work of civilisation, and the great blessing which Russia was to bestow upon barbarous and fanatic Central Asia.

It was only in 1869, when the outposts of the Czar had reached the Oxus, that a considerable amount of uneasiness began to prevail in the optimistic circles of Great Britain. Prince Gort-schakoff having been asked by Lord Clarendon about the ulterior plans of Russia, gave full assur-ance that his sovereign, the Czar, looked upon Af-ghanistan as completely outside the sphere within which Russia might be called upon to exercise her influence. For a certain time this restriction of the Muscovite sphere was faithfully observed; the Cabinet of St. Petersburg abstained from crossing the Oxus, in the north of Afghanistan; but four years later, nevertheless, she crossed the same river in the north of Khiva. After she declared war against the last-named country, England, alarmed at the magnitude of the preparations, again ventured to modestly ask what this meant. The answer of Russia was to the effect that the expedition dispatched against Khiva would be but a very little one; it would consist of simply four and a half battalions, with the purpose merely and solely to punish acts of brigandage, it being very far from the intentions of the Czar to take possession of Khiva, and that positive orders had been issued to the contrary. This little army consisting of four and a half battalions, consisted in reality of 53 companies of infantry, 25 sotnias of Cossacks, 54 guns, 6 mor-tars, 2 mitrailleuses, 5 rocket divisions, and 19,200 camels, with a complement of about 14,000 men.

F

The British statesmen of the day, believing obstinately in the story of four and a half battalions, did not find the shadow of anything suspicious in Russia's doings, and when the ambassador of the Khan of Khiva appeared at Simla, where he was sent to implore the assistance of the British, he was told by the then Governor-General, Lord Northbrook, that the Queen was exceedingly sorry for the dispute which had arisen between the Khan and the Russian Czar, and that the best the Khivans could do was to make peace with the Russian Emperor and submit to his dictation.

Well, Khiva submitted; Russia got her foot on the left bank of the Oxus, and, in spite of all self-delusions, the uneasiness of England about Russian coterminousness with Afghanistan grew apace. The intention of safe-guarding the limits of the country intervening between England and Russia was in existence, but not the adequate will and power to obtain a desirable solution. Whilst walking in the avenues of Baden-Baden, Lord Clarendon and Prince Gortschakoff were quite happy to stumble over the new idea of a neutral zone to be made out of Afghanistan, a sort of buffer which was sure to prevent any future collisions; for his Majesty, the Czar, gave his sacred promises to fully respect the neutrality of the country of the Afghans; and English optimists, asking for nothing better than a loophole to escape through, were quite happy at this arrangement.

But the Czar is at the far distance in the north; and his representative at Tashkend happened to have such notions of Afghan neutrality as were entirely different from those of his master. Whilst the English were enjoying the full beatitude of the peaceful arrangement made with their northern rival, this very representative of the Czar was indefatigable in sending secret missions and correspondences to the Emir of Kabul, in which the latter was told of the great interest the people of Russia took in his fate, and particularly how they pitied him for having become the victim of English despotism, treachery, and egotism. Of these Russian *billets doux* but very little has transpired in Europe; but their effect was clearly and unmistakably visible in the behaviour of the late Shir Ali Khan, a prince of tolerably good disposition, and certainly far superior to the present ruler of Afghanistan, but who, soured by the irresolute policy of the Viceroy of India at the time he was struggling hard for his throne against various competitors, just wanted the above-mentioned secret encouragement and this continual goading from Tashkend in order to become the declared enemy of Great Britain, as he afterwards proved.

We have no space here to dwell at any length

F 2

upon the main causes of the second Afghan war; nor shall we enter into the discussion of whether it was the short-sightedness of the Conservatives in England, or the rashness of Lord Lytton, which precipitated that bloody campaign. But we cannot abstain from remarking that Shir Ali was by no·means the innocent lamb he is represented to be by the Liberal politicians of Great Britain. Left to his own fate through the principles of "masterly inactivity," and getting, through his own efforts, upon the *musnud* of Kabul, the subsidies he got in the shape of presents from Calcutta were utterly inefficient to make this man a staunch ally of England. He was always sulky and always hankering after an increase in the subsidies, for he was more greedy than the rest of the Afghans; and, having been secretly spurred and pushed from Tashkend, it was but quite natural that the good understanding between him and Great Britain should have turned out a failure, that the meetings at Amballah and Simla proved unsuccessful, and that the second Afghan war was an unavoidable consequence of this long tension.

The history of the arrival of the Russian mission under Stolyetoff at Kabul, and the refusal of the Emir to receive the British mission, are· too fresh in memory to require any reiteration.

Through the secret correspondence discovered in the citadel of the Afghan capital, we even got a copy of the treaty concluded between Shir Ali and General Kauffmann, an official document embodying ten stipulations, and evidently showing that Russia had for a long time back prepared the ground for her dealings with Afghanistan, in spite of the officially-acknowledged neutrality of that country. Of course, in excuse of these secret dealings Russia says she was compelled to do so in consequence of the appearance of the British fleet before Constantinople during the late Turko-Russian war. She now feigns perfect innocence; but who in the world would not look through these crafty machinations, and become convinced · by these indubitable facts of the unparalleled treachery brought into action against England?

And, strange to say, there still is a class of politicians who do not view matters in this light. The war against Afghanistan went on with varied fortune; the country was subdued nearly as far as to the Hilmend. Shir Ali Khan died, and was succeeded by his son, Yakoob Khan; and he again had just been deposed from his throne and interned in Murree, for having connived at the treacherous murder of Sir Louis Cavagnari and the English ·mission at Kabul, when soon afterwards, in the spring of 1880, the Liberals returned to power in England, and soon began to change entirely the line of policy pursued by their predecessors. As is pretty well known, the main and principal aim of the Conservative Ministry in going to war against Afghanistan, was to secure a scientific frontier in the place of the former unscientific, *i.e.*, unsafe, and unreliable one. The scientific frontier may be designated, if we say that it was to have comprised a line of country extending from the Kheiber to Quettah, including the Kheiber and Mishni passes, as well as other defiles, leading from India into Afghanistan, together with the Kuram, Sibi, and Pishin, in order to obtain, as Sir Henry Rawlinson very justly remarked, a strong, friendly, and independent power in the north-west of India, without being obliged to accept any crushing liabilities in return. By the treaty of Gundámuk, this scientific frontier was secured. Kabul, with the whole of Afghanistan, reaching to the left bank of the Oxus, had to fall back into the hands of the Emir, and the retention or evacuation of Kandahar was the only question yet left to be decided. The Liberals not only made up their minds very soon to evacuate the last-named place, but were foolish enough to give up the whole scientific frontier, so dearly bought by the precious lives of thousands, and at the cost of more than £20,000,000 of money. In order to

obliterate any trace of the work done by their predecessors, they tore up the rails laid down in the
direction of Pishin, forsook all those Afghans who
had joined the cause of the English, and exhibited
an almost incomprehensible fanatical desire to anni-
hilate even the slightest results obtained by the
second Afghan war.

As a foreigner I must naturally abstain from
entering too deeply into the intricacies of English
party-life; but with all my firm resolution I cannot
suppress the remark that, if the Liberal politicians of
Great Britain had adopted up to this point the policy
of "masterly inactivity" against aggressive Russia,
they have since changed that device into one of
"masterly imbecility," for whilst they were evacuating
Kandahar, against the clear and expressed opinions of
military and political authorities, such as Lord Napier
of Magdala, General Roberts, Colonel Malleson, General Sir Edward Hamley, Lord Lytton, Sir Richard
Temple, and a host of others, their Russian friend was
steadily making his way across the Turkoman country
towards the Paropamisus mountains. Mr. Charles
Marvin is, therefore, quite right in illustrating this
fact in his above quoted book as follows :—"Just
before the evacuation of Kandahar took place, a
clever caricature was published in Russia, entitled,
'England and Russia in Central Asia.' This repre-

sented two feet; one, English shod, stepping off a piece of ground marked 'Afghanistan,' and another, encased in a big Russian boot, advancing closely upon it, with the evident intention of administering a kick to the retiring party." Of the suicidal policy of evacuating Kandahar we shall speak hereafter, but will only add by the way, that the Kandahar people themselves were no less averse to the evacuation than the English public at large. Admitting that there have been, and always will be, fanatics in Mohammedan communities, it must not be lost sight of that a large majority of Kandaharees, and particularly the Tadjik and Parsivan portion, are a trading and industrious people, who preferred the settled rule, order, and justice, introduced by the English, to the despotism of rapacious Afghan Serdars; and they not only regretted the departure of the British, but I remember having read a kasideh (poem) in praise of their new rulers, and bewailing their having been left by them.

CHAPTER VI.

HAVING succeeded in undoing entirely the work of their predecessors, the party in power in England since 1880 have been afforded ample opportunity to become convinced of the gross mistakes into which they had rushed. But, alas! blindness, a great misfortune with single individuals, is certainly far more disastrous in the case of a large body, and, particularly if that large body is entrusted with the conduct of the affairs of a powerful State such as Great Britain.

Whilst publicly clinging, with rare obstinacy worthy of a better cause, to the soundness of their views, they seemed to have been secretly very often roused from their slumbers of delusive security. As the Russian columns proceeded along the Kubbet mountains, in the north of Persia, the leading statesmen in London were more than once seized by feelings of restlessness. Interpellations, couched in polite and considerate language, were sent to St. Petersburg, where particular care was taken not to offend the dear friends on the Thames. Such polite but meaningless answers were vouchsafed at the time when Russia rectified her frontier on the Gurgan with Persia. Of a similar tenor was the excuse sent, after the Russian victory at Geok-Tepe; and who does not remember the glorious tidings Sir Charles Dilke brought to the House of Commons, announcing that the Czar, in order to allay the apprehensions of the British, had recalled General Skobeleff from the scene of his heroic exploits, and that henceforward not a single step would be made towards the east, for it was solely and exclusively the intention of the Czar to chastise the reckless Turkoman robbers, and to put an end to that horrible man-stealing occupation of these lawless tribes. Humanitarian England exulted with joy thereat, and those who ventured to view things in a different light were stigmatised as reckless barbarians. A short pause set in ; but with the insatiable earth-hunger of Russia, who, as we related, very soon stretched out a feeler towards Merv, the party could, unfortunately, but a very short time enjoy their rest.

At the Russian plea that the last named place had voluntarily submitted, even the staunchest believers in Muscovite promises began to shake their heads. Merv was the last straw which broke the back of the British ministerial camel, and poor Sir Edward Thornton in St. Petersburg had the worst of it, for he had to keep up an incessant running from the Czar to Giers and from Giers to the Czar. At one moment he got a despatch from London to ask for an explanation concerning the seizure of Merv. The Czar gives a decided denial to the statement, vowing that he never had the slightest intention of taking Merv, and that he will never take it. Sir Edward telegraphs home the reassuring answer of his Russian Majesty; but, on hearing a statement to the contrary from London, he has to inquire again, and now he learns how displeased and angry his Russian Majesty was with his generals on the frontier, who always act in disobedience to his orders, causing so many, many worries to him. The poor Czar is really the most troubled man in the world; but, as a good-natured ruler, he ultimately gives in, and not only retains the object of vexation, but bestows even honours upon those who have trespassed upon his forbearance. This has been the history and process of many Russian annexations in Asia; it would have proved equally efficacious with Merv, had it not been for the fact that this was the last drop which filled to overflowing the cup of Russian lies and breaches of faith. This fact startled even the most optimistic politicians on the Thames. The flood of English diplomatic despatches to St. Petersburg went on swelling, the machinery in Downing Street

was worked at a high steam pressure, and, strange to
say, the anxiously looked for explanation had not yet
arrived when Liberal England awoke to another
surprise—namely, the seizure of Sarakhs, of a place
which lies beyond the so-called Turkoman country,
and could have nothing to do with the civilising
measures taken against the Turkomans.

I call this new Russian move a surprise, although,
from the very beginning, it must have been patent to
everybody that, having succeeded in annexing the
country north of Persia, she would glide down also
on the eastern frontier of the same country; this all
the more as the tract intervening between Afghanistan and Persia is deservedly called "No man's
land," and, in fact, could not have been designated
as the property of anybody for the last two hundred
years, since when the Turkomans, becoming masters
of the Tedjend and Murghab oases, have used this
intervening track as a highway for their robberies
into the interior of Persia.   Of this fact Russia was
fully aware, even at the outset of her conquering
trips against the Turkomans ; for attentive readers of
Russia's doings in this quarter of the world will
remember the elaborate report General Petrusevitch
made, when Governor of Krasnovodsk, in which
he earnestly advised his Government to thrust a
wedge between Persia and Afghanistan, through the

occupation of this "no man's land;" an advice the
adoption of which soon followed after the conquest of .
Merv, a place ridiculed by a certain class of English
statesmen as a collection of a few mud huts, and
certainly an unworthy object to make the British
public nervous about.

As the country intervening between Herat and
Persia had remained hitherto almost a *terra incognita*,
we shall try to give to the reader, as briefly as
possible, a description of it.   In glancing at this
portion of the map of Asia, the reader will discover two rivers which run in an almost parallel
direction from the east towards the south, and then
suddenly turning towards the north, disappear in
the sands of the Karakum.   One is the Murghab,
which rises in the north slope of the Sefid-Kuh
Mountains, traverses the mountainous district occupied by the Hezares, and enters beyond Maruchak
the plain bordering on the Turkoman country, after
having united with the Khushk beyond Penjdeh at
a place called Pul-i-Khishti, *i.e.*, brick bridge, or as
the Turkomans call it, Dash-Köpri, *i.e.*, stone bridge.
The other river, the Heri-Rud, *i.e.*, Heri river, rises
232 miles east of Herat, flows in a westerly direction,
passing the places of Shekivan, Rusenek, Shebesh, and
Tirpul, and turning near Kuhsan, goes in an almost
northerly direction along the eastern border of Persia,

passing Sarakhs to the so-called Tedjend oasis, where it loses itself in the sands.

Now the country between these two rivers, intersected by other minor rivulets, such as the Kash, the Egri-Goek, the Gurlan-Su, the Khombou-Su (affluents of the Murghab) forms the so-called debatable ground between the Afghans and the Russians, and is really worth the dispute it gives rise to, considering its fame for fertility and the varied productions it is capable of bringing forth. In the southern portion we find the Borkhut Mountain, a prolongation of the Sefid-Kuh, increasing in height as it approaches the Persian frontier, and forming the principal branch by which the Paropamisus is united with the Elburz. Farther up, about thirty-six degrees north, we discover the much lower chain, called by Lessar the Elbirin-Kir, rather a succession of hills stretching to Pul-i-Khatun, whilst the mountainous district through which the Khushk and its tributaries flow, the so-called outskirts of the Paropamisus, are not of a much higher elevation, affording, therefore, full facilities for agricultural purposes—in fact, the whole district may be called arable up to Noruzabad and Sarakhs, where the desert begins.

The climate is very dissimilar in the various portions of the country; it may be called an agreeable one on the whole, excepting for the strong winds,

which generally blow from the north towards the
south, and which gave rise to the whole district
being named in ancient times Badkhyz—*i.e.*, the
place where the wind gets up. The vegetation can,
therefore, be called not only a rich, but even a luxuriant one. Along the banks both of the Heri-Rud
and the Murghab (says Lessar in *The Scottish Geographical Magazine* of May, 1885), "great quantities
of poplars, mulberry trees, willows, and bushes of
various kinds occur, so dense that in many places it is
not only impossible to approach the river on horse-
back, but even to make one's way on foot. Fodder
for horses is everywhere in abundance, and of good
quality. The trees growing there reach no inconsiderable dimensions. . . . . In the district
between the rivers, on the sandy clayey soil, mulberry
trees occur only near the springs, and pistachio trees
are scattered on all the hill-slopes, for the most part
singly, with considerable intervals between."

I can add to what Lessar says, that grain is found
growing richly, if the husbandman be undisturbed
by Turkoman inroads, in the whole country as far
as to the north of the Elbirin-Kir, whilst in the
country to the east—namely, on the banks of the
Khushk and the Murghab—the profuse irrigation
affords ample opportunity for all kind of cultivation, and grain, rice, a great variety of fruit,

thrive with small care. As to the mineral wealth
of the country, the chief production of the plains
is salt, taken from the lakes, which constitutes the
chief export for the Turkoman population; the
quality of the salt is excellent. Other kinds of
mineral wealth may be found in the hills, and
only await utilisation. If I remember well, I
even heard of the existence of coal from one of
the Hezares in the north of Herat; but, at all
events, English geologists travelling just now in
that country, will, I am sure, furnish us the best
information on the subject. In conclusion, I must
remark as to towns, villages, etc., that all the high-
sounding names which have of late come to the notice
of newspaper-readers, either consist of a collection
of a few wretched huts, or mark the ruins of towns
which existed in bygone ages; for, owing to the
constant dangers arising from Turkoman inroads,
the whole country is desolate and deserted, and
there is only the memory of the past which en-
livens the fancy of the traveller. Starting from
the Bundehesh—that curious repository of ancient
Aryan legends, up to the Persian written historical records, reaching to the seventeenth century
—we read in books describing this part of Central
Asia, of the marvels of fertility for which the country
on the banks of the Murghab and Heri-Rud was

noted. But, as I said before, the wanton desolation by wars, the tyrannical despotism of the native rulers, and, above all, the depredations inflicted by reckless Turkoman robbers, have deprived the country of its splendour, and have made it naked and bare like the desert in the north.

It is therefore quite superfluous to remark that Russia had a sharp eye when she directed her steps towards this country, and when she began to use it as a wedge between Persia and Afghanistan;—a wedge through which she will be able to extend, without any difficulty, her line of conquest towards Herat. In former times, want of geographical information induced us to believe that these out-runners of the Paropamisus Mountain form an impassable barrier to the traveller coming from the west, although nothing like this has occurred to the student of Oriental history in reading of the marches made by various armies, from Merv and from Persia, towards Herat. Quite recently that imaginary barrier has utterly disappeared. We know that the highest pass does not reach beyond 900 feet, and the traveller could drive with great ease a calesh, four-in-hand, from Sarakhs to Herat. The passes leading across the Borkhut Mountain, as well as across the Elbirin-Kir, are very numerous, and present no difficulty to the invader.

G

It was during the time that Russia was preparing for the march into this above-described "no man's land," the evident sign of which preparation became visible in the seizure of Sarakhs, that the interchange of diplomatic notes between the Cabinets of London and St. Petersburg went on uninterruptedly. Whether the Liberal statesmen were incensed against their so-called dear friend, for having over and over again violated his given promises, it would be difficult to decide; for there are, even now, statesmen in Great Britain who could swear to the undoubted honesty of Russia. But the fact is that, even while acknowledging the legality of Russia's advances, there were, even amongst the inveterate optimists, men enough who put to themselves the question, "quousque?" and who, entertained in the idea of exacting from Russia an ultimate limit of her extension, hoped to guarantee thus against all eventual collision. Russia, polite as she usually is, conceded at once the desire of her friends on the Thames, and it was settled that a Frontier Delimitating Commission should be appointed from both sides, in order to fix the boundaries between Afghanistan and Russia, from Sarakhs to Khodja-Salih, on the Oxus, and by laying out the variously coloured frontier marks on the long line, running beyond 300 miles, the goodly optimistic politicians expected to disarm

Russia at once, and to make hostilities disappear for ever.

Of course the opportunity was hurriedly grasped by the English, the Frontier Delimitating Commission was appointed, and Sir Peter Lumsden, a member of the India Council, and an officer of thirty-seven years' standing, was put at the head of it. Sir Peter Lumsden, who took part in the engagements of the English in China, in various parts of India and the adjacent countries, and who had acted besides as a member of the special Military Commission to Afghanistan in 1857—58, was decidedly the proper man in the right place, fully qualified for his task by multifarious experiences in border affairs, by sound judgment, and by his straightforward and honest British character. A second commissioner was appointed in the person of Colonel Patrick Stewart, equally capable and honest, and particularly conspicuous for his pluck and patriotic zeal. This was the man who, in the disguise of an Armenian horse-dealer, entered in 1880 the Turkoman frontier, and kept up his incognito so cleverly that Mr. O'Donovan, the correspondent of the *Daily News*, and the famous explorer of Merv, who met the colonel on the frontier of Persia, could not discover in him his countryman, although living with him in the same place for three weeks. Colonel Stewart having been

G 2

employed after his journey as a political agent in
Khaf, a Persian town in the west of Herat, and
possessing the best information on the debatable
country, was, therefore a good acquisition for the
said Commission. Another officer was Lieut.-
Colonel J. West Ridgway, Foreign Under Secretary
to the Government of India. He was entrusted with
the lead of the Indian section of the Delimitating
Commission, and his march from Nushkhi, across the
desert, to the Hilmend, proves him a sagacious and
circumspect officer. I must mention, besides, Major
Napier, an officer famous for his instructive report
on the northern frontiers of Persia, and Mr. Condie
Stephen, second secretary to the legation at Teheran,
whom I had occasion personally to meet, and whose
versatility in the Russian and Persian languages,
really surprised me. I ought to say, too, a few
words about the native Indian and Afghan members of the commission, but we cannot dwell on
such details at any length. Suffice it that the whole
commission, having to be protected against unexpected attacks on the Turkomán frontier, was furnished with an escort composed of 200 cavalry of
the 11th Bengal Lancers, but known as Probyn's
Horse, and of 250 infantry, the entire commission
making altogether 35 Europeans, and 1,300 natives.
Starting from different points, the Indian section,

under Ridgway, reached Herat on the 17th of November, after having traversed over 767 miles from Quettah to Kuhsan; whilst the smaller portion, consisting of Sir Peter Lumsden and the leading officers of his staff, arrived on the 19th of November, after a journey of 1,000 miles from Resht, on the Caspian, through Khorassan, and met their countrymen at Kuhsan.

The English Delimitating Commission, on arriving on the spot, was no little surprised at finding no trace of their Russian colleagues—namely, of General Zelenoy, the Russian Commissioner-in-Chief, to whom were subordinated Major Alikhanoff, M. Lessar, and other Russian officers familiar with the frontier. Instead of their colleagues, they found, however, at Pul-i-Khatun, forty miles south of Sarakhs, a Russian picket of Cossacks gazing at the English comers, as if to ask of them, " What have you got to look for in Russian territory ? " Now we can readily imagine that this first rebuff was sufficient to convince Sir Peter Lumsden of the utter futility of the task before him, and that the English gentlemen had rather a bad foretaste of the work entrusted to them. It must be borne in mind that it was upon the Sarakhs Khodja-Salih line that the frontier rectification was to take place. For we read in the Blue Book (" Central Asia, No. 1," 1884), that M. de Giers, with a view to preventing disturbances on the borders of Afghanistan, considered it to be of great importance that the boundary of that country from Khodja-Salih to the Persian frontier, in the neighbourhood of Sarakhs, should be formally and definitely laid down, and that he had instructed Prince Lobanoff to endeavour to induce her Majesty's Government to agree to the adoption of measures for that purpose. If such were Russian measures in 1882, we may well ask what were the reasons of that sudden change, and why was the frontier line pushed down southwards forty miles to Pul-i-Khatun, and subsequently another forty miles southward to the Zulfikar Pass on the Heri-Rud? The answer will be very easily found if we consider that, during the last two years, the English having entered upon the venturesome undertaking in Egypt, and having become thoroughly immersed in troubles in the Soudan, were deemed by the politicians on the Neva as really incapable of resistance, and easily to be tampered with according to Russia's heart's desire. It is certainly one of the worst tricks that has ever been played by diplomacy, when we consider that Russia, availing herself of the embarrassments of the Liberal Government on the Thames, was unconscionable enough to pitch into that very Mr. Gladstone who was the author and upholder of Russian sympathies in England, who swore by the sincerity of the

Czar, and who was fated now to bitterly expiate his Russian proclivities. Of course sentimentality, unknown in politics, had never a home in St. Petersburg, and Russia, disregarding all previous promises relating to the frontier points, thought proper to annex as much as she could, and by using the device of Prince Bismarck, namely, " *Beati possidentes*," to fix a line wherever favourable circumstances afforded the best opportunity.

Apart from this move to the south, on the banks of the Heri-Rud, Russia had begun simultaneously to push on towards that portion of the Murghab river which was the indisputable possession of the Afghans, namely, to Penjdeh, in order to secure a firm footing in the cultivable regions of the Paropamisus outskirts, after having crossed the desert from Merv to the last-named place. The plan as to this portion of Afghanistan had already become ripe in 1884, for, after the successful termination of the comedy of voluntary submission at Merv, vague rumours were spread about concerning an equally voluntary submission of the Sarik Turkomans living in and around Penjdeh, and, in fact, certain elders of the said tribes presented themselves at Ashkabad, and, after having obtained presents from General Komaroff, deposited their oaths of fidelity to the Czar, without the slightest right, however, of representing their own nation, as

we afterwards learned.   To Russia this farce was sufficient to make her come forward with claims upon
Penjdeh.   Major Alikhanoff, entrusted with the
occupation of Penjdeh, tried several times to get
possession of the place, and having found there in
June, 1884, a strong Afghan garrison, and seeing that
the Sarik had not the slightest notion of the so-called
voluntary submission to the Czar, for they were ready
to attack the Cossacks in company with the Afghans,
he saw himself compelled to retire upon Merv, without giving up, however, the hope of a future successful annexation.

Sir Peter Lumsden, together with the members of
the Delimitating Commission, on seeing how totally
different the state of things on the spot was from
what he had reason to expect in London, and finding
how difficult it was to carry out the instructions given
to him by the Liberal ministry, at once entered upon
a lively exchange of despatches with his superiors,
and pointed out that there must be something wrong
about the whole question of frontier rectification.
We, the distant lookers-on, felt from the beginning a
distrust of the whole concern.   The writer of these
lines was one of the first who ridiculed the whole
affair of future delimitation, in a paper published in
the *National Review* of November, 1884.   He styled
the whole thing one of the most ridiculous farces

ever played in politics, and concluded the above-
mentioned paper by saying : " For whilst public
opinion in England is lulled by these palliatives into
the torpor of security, Russia has the finest opportunity, backed by this illusory frontier-line, to prepare
herself in silence for that leap which will deal her
death-blow to Great Britain, great and powerful as
she still is at this moment." A few weeks later, the
same writer, feeling his patience exhausted at the
designedly dilatory steps of Russia, drew the attention
of the British public, in a letter addressed to the
editor of *The Times*, to the ignominious forbearance
shown by the British Cabinet in permitting the
Commission to be kept waiting for months, camped
beneath the inclement sky of the Paropamisan winter,
and explained that he discovered an intentional insult
in the fact of the British Lion being made to ante-
chamber at the Russian Bear's.

This letter had the desired effect upon the English
public. The great majority of the English press
joined in reproaching the Government for its unjustifiable and undignified forbearance. Questions were
repeatedly put in the House of Commons, the diplomatic correspondence between London and St. Peters-
berg grew quicker and more excited, assuming a tone
of asperity, and it was then only that the question
began to show itself in its true and genuine shape,

betraying, at the same time, the serious importance of
the claims put forward by Russia.   First of all we
got to hear that the cabinet of St. Petersburg had
made up its mind to form a strictly ethnical, and not
a geographical frontier, being the very cabinet which,
eleven years before, had said in the famous circular of
Prince Gortschakoff in 1864, that she had a strong
belief in " *les conditions géographiques et politiques qui
sont fixes et permanentes.*"   This was, at all events, a
very strange obliviousness in the matter of principles ;
an obliviousness quite suited, however, to the actual
purposes in view ; for, whilst on the banks of the
Yaxartes the frontier line between Tashkend fully
justified the adoption of a geographical method, the
circumstances on the Murghab were of quite a different
nature, and necessitated the adoption of the ethnical
method instead, for the simple reason that Russia,
anxious to get at the cultivable region of Afghanistan,
had to put forward her claim upon the Sarik population.   It was announced in the usual high-sounding
phrases, that in order to tranquillise the whole Turkoman country, it had become unavoidably necessary
that not a single member of that family should be
left out, for should the Sarik in the east, and the
Salor in the south, remain independent, or under
Afghan rule, their predatory habits would cause dis-
turbance, and highly aggravate, nay, render impossible

a settled rule in Merv, and in the Tedjend oasis. What very strange logicians these Russians are! Ten years ago, when reducing the Yomut tribe, they did not entertain the slightest scruple at leaving a large portion of that people under the Persian sway, and, satisfied with the geographical frontier of the Gurgan, the idea of an ethnical frontier did not so much as enter their minds. But, good gracious! times and circumstances change. Now, the ethnical frontier had come to the fore, and seemed to them the only sound basis for an arrangement. At all events a ludicrous idea, for whilst the geographical frontier is steady and immovable, the ethnical one, based upon the roving habits of nomadic and plundering Turkomans, is of a pre-eminently shifting character, but exactly suiting Russia, who was also bent upon shifting the limits of her possessions towards Afghanistan, and endeavouring to get as near as possible to the roads which would bring her the more quickly to the Gate of India.

Nearly four months now elapsed, spent in continual discussion, carried on partly between the two Cabinets, partly between the press of the countries. What the contents of these despatches may have been, we, uninitiated mortals, have no right to inquire into; but with reference to the enunciations of the press, we have seen that the question mainly turned on the

legal aspect of the Russian or Afghan claim to the
debatable country, the former being very naturally
backed by Russian papers, and the latter, with the
exception of one Russianised paper, by the press of
Great Britain. We really wonder at English statesmen
and English journalists, that in spite of their ample
experience of Russian mendacity and unexampled
arrogance, they took the trouble to discuss the legal
view of the question, knowing very well that, in the
ultimate end, the Russian principle of "might is
right," was sure to carry the point. The arguments
advanced by Russia in reference to Penjdeh, rested
mainly upon the assumption that the Afghans had
but quite recently taken possession of Penjdeh,
inhabited by the Sarik Turkomans, and that this
place had always been looked upon as an integral
part of the Turkoman country. Now this is, to use
the mildest expression, the most insolent lie ever
invented, for not only does the geographical position
of Penjdeh speak against such an assumption, but
also all the available historical records laid down in
the works of Oriental writers. In the Tarikhi Djihan
Kusha, composed by Djuveini, in the second half of
the thirteenth century, we read of the Badghis as
belonging to Herat, and handed over, afterwards, to
the Chihar Aimaks. Later on we meet with statements to the same effect made by the historian of

Timur, as well as in the reports of the historiographers of the last Timurides. Last and not least, we may mention that the name of Penjdeh is strictly Persian, meaning five villages; the name is the last Persian nomenclature in this direction, for farther to the north, the topography in the desert is entirely and exclusively of Turkish origin. As to the Afghan claim, justified by the historical record of the recent past, we may quote a passage of a letter published in the *Times of India*, June 2, by the special correspondent of that paper with the Boundary Commission, in the contents of which we shall only correct the orthography of the proper names, not easily manageable by a non-orientalist authority:

"It is probably through some subtle quibbling over the Herat and Kabul kingdoms, and cunning argument as to the period and extent of Afghan domination in Herat, that the Russians have come to convince themselves, and persuade many others, that Penjdeh is not, and has not been, in possession of the Afghans and a portion of Afghan territory. We have a map of the Afghan, or rather, Herat kingdom in the time of Yar Mohammed, prepared by Todd. This map both shows Penjdeh and Pul-i-Khatun to have been in possession of Herat at that period. The Russian officials on this side of Turkestan must have seen the watch-towers up to Pul-i-Khatun. These raid observatories were built by Wazeer Ameer Kildy Khan in the time of Shah Zeman—say, some sixty years ago. Since the death of Nadir Shah, the district of Penjdeh and Badghis has unquestionably belonged to the Afghans, whether power gravitated towards Herat, or Kabul, or Kandahar. About sixty years ago Penjdeh was inhabited by Djemshidis and Huzaras. When these sections of the Aimak family left, the Ersari Turkoman came and paid tribute to the Afghan Government. After the Ersari a few Salor Turkomans arrived and settled. At this period a Naib of the Afghan Government always resided in Penjdeh. On the departure of the Djemshidis and Huzaras from Penjdeh, the Afghan Government appear to have recovered the revenue of the district through the Huzara chief of Kila Nau. The modern history of the district is embodied in the relations between the Sariks and Afghans. Some eight and twenty years ago the Sarik moved down from Merv, and pressed out the weaker elements attracted around Penjdeh. The Sarik having moved down to Penj-deh, and seized the fertile banks of the Khushk and Murghab, near their united waters, the Ersari departed to the Oxus eastwards, where they prospered, and are still prospering, and only a few hundred families of the Salor remained at Pul-i-Khishti and Kila Nau. The Ersari in physique are considered by many to be

superior to either Tekke or Sarik; they are fairer and
taller men than the other Turkomans we have seen.
A very clear record of the revenue relations between
the settlers at Penjdeh and the Afghan Government
exists. The obligation of acknowledging their fealty
in the payment of revenue, appears never to have
been avoided. *Zukat* in cattle and corn has always
been paid. The amount of revenue from Penjdeh
must have fluctuated with the influence and stability
of the Government at Kabul or Herat; but at all
times *zukat* appears to have been acknowledged. The
succession of Afghan Governors at Penjdeh estab-
lishes the chain of connection: it is scarcely necessary
to refer to those Governors, whose period of office was
not memorable for any remarkable works, nor connected with any memorable events. As long a time
ago as sixty years a Djemshidi represented the Afghan Government at Penjdeh—Dervish Khan was
then Governor." To Merv Penjdeh never did belong,
it always formed the last station of the district of
Herat, and the Russian claim is, therefore, from every
point of view unfounded and unjust.

As to the Russian claims to the country south of
Sarakhs, they are the easier refuted, and proved a
wanton encroachment, if we consider that the Heri-
Rud was, from immemorial times, the very frontier-
line between Persia and Herat, and that even at such

periods, when the kings of Iran possessed themselves
of the last-named town, the Heri-Rud was looked
upon as the border of the Herat district, whilst the
left bank was accounted to belong to the district of
Meshed. And what should we say of the ethnical
rights of Russia, considering that the Sarik Turkomans belonged, in the fifteenth century already, to
Herat, and are called even by the Tartar historian,
Abulghazi Khan, *Herat Turkmeni*, in contra-distinc-
tion to the Merv Turkmeni. And why should not
we point to the utter want of consistency shown by
Russia in asking the Sariks and their country as an
integral portion of the Turkoman world, whereas
she did not claim the Yomuts, on the left bank of the
Gurgan, and the Salors living in Zorabad, on Persian
territory? Indeed, it would be wasting time if we
were to dilate any longer upon the shallow and
insolent pretensions of Russia, and we must repeatedly
express our astonishment that English statesmen took
the trouble to seriously combat the claims put forward
in St. Petersburg.

Russia being perfectly clear, in her own mind,
upon what she was bent, did not spare any pains to
impress upon the Liberal cabinet the justness of her
assertions, and in order to achieve this, she despatched
M. Lessar to London, as an assistant to M. de Staal;
the same M. Lessar who had explored the country

around Herat, and had been the chief coadjutor in planning the mischievous policy against England. Now against M. de Staal, in company with M. Lessar, poor Lord Kimberley and Lord Granville were certainly an unequal match; but, nevertheless, the consultations went on, and in order to ensure the result of these consultations, an arrangement or an agreement was entered into, that the Russians and Afghans should maintain their positions in the debatable country during that time, or at least so long as the deliberations in London had not come to an end. Russia pledged her word, on the condition that no untoward event should occur; and, as the occurrence of such untoward events rested in her own hands, she was clever and mischievous enough to bring on the famous catastrophe of the 30th of March, in which, as is pretty well-known, nearly 700 Afghans were slaughtered in cold blood on the banks of the Khushk. This incident, which forms even now, as I am writing, the subject of discussion between the two Governments, was, as Sir Peter Lumsden is reported to have said to *The Times* correspondent at Vienna, an unprovoked and utterly unjustifiable aggression on the part of General Komaroff, an act premeditated a long time ago, and committed in direct violation of all international law; an assertion which is tolerably justified by the fact that the

H

result of this untoward event was reaped by Russia, inasmuch as she took possession of the much-coveted Penjdeh and holds it even now.

We need not be astonished at the extraordinary sensation, mixed with bitter feelings of animosity against Russia, the bloody affair on the Khushk has produced in England. Not only Conservative, but also Liberal politicians, unanimous in their condemnation of Russian treachery, were loudly crying for war. All England was ablaze; only the Liberal Ministry kept cool, and, in their indefatigable zeal to discover the real cause of that mischief, they happily found out that the Muscovite lambs were again innocent, that they were pressed upon to fight against the Afghans; nay, they went even farther, and, immolating the good name of their own country-man, they were not ashamed to come forward with the assertion that it was the harshness of Sir Peter Lumsden and his party which had hastened the ill-fated event.

This escape, the greatest blot which has ever stained the character of British statesmen, having been found, the negotiations went on again un-interruptedly, and are going on even now as I write these lines, for no definite information is extant about the frontier regulations between Russia and Afghan-istan, and all that has oozed out hitherto consists of the fact that Russia is to remain in possession of Penjdeh, in spite of all the geographical, historical, and ethnical arguments speaking against her, and that only her position on the Heri-Rud still remains open to discussion. Referring to this part of the question, we hear that the Czar has been kind enough to give up the Zulfikar Pass, that he is ready to fix the most southerly point of his frontier in the north of the last-named place, and that this frontier line is now to run from the Heri-Rud, skirting the Elbirin-Kir in the south, and including the Er-Oilan salt lakes; it will cross the Murghab south of Penjdeh, and thence to the Oxus. The details of this delimitation, being hitherto unknown, and requiring a good deal of time until they will be finally settled, we may now well consider the results which Russia has obtained in this protracted contest, by stating at once *that the unheard of short-sightedness of British statesmen has handed over to her the very keys with which she can now open, at her leisure, the gate of India; for she is in full possession of all the ways which can bring her to Herat in a comparatively short time and without any difficulty whatever.*

CHAPTER VII.

In full accordance with our opinion are also the views expressed, quite recently, by competent military authorities of Great Britain. Amongst others we shall quote the following portion extracted from a paper published in *The Times*, (May 26, 1885), under the title "Our Strategical Position in Asia with regard to Russia," from the pen of a writer whose modesty in remaining anonymous, is only equalled by the rare ability with which he handles his subject.

"But it is unnecessary to dilate on the importance of Herat and the danger to us of its falling into hostile hands. On that importance and danger, all military experts, with few exceptions, are unanimous and positive. Indeed, the measure of its value is afforded by the eager desire of Russia to obtain it. With the frontier line conceded to her, she not only has the town itself within her grasp, but even without it she is practically the master of the whole of the vast resources of the district; and it is the district, rather

than the mere fortress, which it is her object to seize,
and which will be valuable to her.   Even, however,
if she contents herself for the moment with a line, the
extremities of which, as regards the Badghis, are
points a few miles to the north of Maruchak and
Zulficar, she will still possess a large district, part of
which is already cultivated, most of the remainder
being capable of being shortly rendered very pro-
ductive.   She will possess a substantial slice of the
place d'assemblée which she covets, and can in the
course of a fortnight seize the whole of the remainder; for we may assume that in the course of
the next twelve months the railway from the Caspian
will be completed as far as the Murghab, if not up to
the Oxus.   Then she will be in a position to reinforce
the troops occupying the line Zulficar—Penjdeh by
troops from the Caucasus at the rate of a division a
week.   It is idle to talk about leaving to the
Afghans this or that pass in the Borkhut or Paropamisus ranges, if the Russians possess all the roads
which lead to them.   The passes are numerous, but
most of them are easy to force, and probably there
are numerous by-paths by which they could be
turned.   The so-called impassable ranges are not
impassable at all, and can be crossed, according to
Lessar, at a height of 900 feet above the plain.   A
few distances will enable the reader to appreciate the

position.   From Sarakhs, *viâ* the Valley of the Heri-
Rud to Herat is 202 miles ; from Zulficar to Herat,
about 142 miles by the same road ; from Zulficar to
Kuhsan is 86 miles ; from Kuhsan to Herat is 62
miles ; from Sarakhs to Penjdeh, 100 miles ; from
Zulficar to Penjdeh, 90 miles ; from Akrobat to
Herat, 80 miles ; from Penjdeh and from Bala
Murghab about 140 miles ; from Penjdeh to
Maruchak, 28 miles ; from Maruchak to Bala
Murghab, 28 miles.   Thus it will be seen that at the
rate of twelve miles a day—a low average, considering
the shortness of the whole distance and that the
Russians are good marchers—a Russian division
could reach Herat *in twelve days from Penjdeh, from
Akrobat in seven days, and from Zulficar in eight days.*
Sir Edward Hamley estimates the time required at
fourteen days from Penjdeh, and from Zulficar at
ten or eleven days.   I have reason to believe that
the distances are not accurately stated in either maps
or itineraries ; but it is safe to assert that a Russian
division of all arms could, by forced marches, reach
Herat from the nearest point of what will probably
be the new Russian frontier in eight days, and that
cavalry and Cossack batteries could do so in four days.
When the railway shall have been completed to
Sarakhs, the distance by marching from thence will
be three weeks at the most."

Having spoken in our previous remarks, at some length, on the district of Herat, we shall now turn our attention to the town itself, and try to prove the truth of the old saying that Herat really is the gate of India, an object in view which I hope to attain by publishing here the largest portion of my own paper bearing on the subject, which I read before the "Society of Arts" in London on the 1st of May, 1885, where I was glad to see a distinguished audience, including leading statesmen and ministers :—

"To speak to-day about Herat, in the face of the numerous and important literary manifestations called forth by the keen interest felt in the subject, is, to say the least of it, an undertaking as hazardous as a visit to that city would have proved a few years ago. I cannot, therefore, offer you much that is novel; and if, nevertheless, I come before you with a lecture on Herat, I do so actuated by the hope of being able to find, after all, a thing or two in my experience, derived from personal observation, which may claim your interest under the present circumstances. In Herat I passed six weeks, and sad weeks they were. Without money or sympathy, and without any hope of speedy relief, I spent many, many hours in my cell in the dilapidated caravansary, pondering on the importance of that city and its past

and future.   Since that time I have been frequently
taken back by my theoretical studies to the same
spot.   On my return to Europe I found that the
English politicians of that day were strongly inclined
towards optimism, and disposed to dispute with me
about the importance of Herat, and I consequently
published, in 1869, an essay entitled ' Herat, and the
Central-Asiatic Question,' in which I stoutly maintained the claim of Herat to the title of the ' Gate
of India.'   Sixteen years have passed since.   The
importance of Herat continued to be looked on as an
empty phrase for some time afterwards, until at last,
in our own days, the conviction has forced itself
upon all mankind that Alexander the Great, who
founded that city in 327 B.C., was not so bad a politician after all; and that the subsequent conquerors
of India were only obeying the logic of facts in considering the possession of that place as a *sine quâ non*
of their success in the south.

"Herat is in truth, for a variety of reasons, a
place of unusual importance, and amongst them are
the agricultural, commercial, ethnic, and strategic
advantages possessed by it, which I shall proceed to
point out.   Whilst I was still in the desert with my
companions, to the north of the Paropamisus Mountains, they were never tired of repeating to me:—
'Have but patience!   We are nearing the blessed

land; we are going to Herat. There the bread is
whiter than the moon, the water sweeter than sugar.
You can get there a pot of cream for a farthing, the
roast lamb there is deliciously savoury, and the most
exquisite varieties of fruit can be got for a mere
trifle.' I arrived in Herat during the autumn, just
after the city had passed through a siege of three
years. The entire place was a shocking heap of
ruins, the environs had been despoiled of all the
trees, and yet for all that, when I ventured into the
more secluded valleys, and saw and tasted of the
rich variety of the products to be found there, I could
not help marvelling at the wonderful productiveness
of the soil. I discovered that the statements of the
geographers of antiquity were by no means exagger-
ated, and that the glowing accounts of my fellow-
travellers were strictly true. The soil of Herat is of
incredible fertility, and, with the exception of the
cultivated oasis in the territory of Zerefshan, there is
not another spot in the whole of the Asiatic world,
between Siberia and India, which could vie for productiveness with those valleys of the Paropamisus.
The wheat ripens in June, and ranks in quality with
the so-called Jerusalem wheat of Khiva. The grapes
are much more palatable than the celebrated kinds
coming from Bokhara, and superior even to the
Tchaush grapes from the environs of Smyrna. The

pears and apples are better than those so highly prized
in Asia, known as Nathenzians, and the mutton
much more savoury than that of Shiraz and Kara-
man, which is saying a great deal. The inhabitants
of Herat have good wool in abundance for the textiles
required for their raiment, wood for their buildings,
and a great variety of minerals which are only awaiting
development. They not only have enough for themselves, but they are also supplying the surrounding
country. Thus has the rice of Herat always been
one of the chief articles of food of the Turkomans of
Merv, and the Hezares in the east; whilst the
fabrics of Herat, such as carpets, furs, and different
varieties of leather, were being exported by them far
and wide. I must make here particular mention of
the fact, that not only in my time, and during this
and the preceding century has Herat been a ruin,
but ever since the decline of the Timurides, Herat
became the bone of contention among the Persians,
Afghans, Uzbegs, Turkomans, and Hezares. Peace
but rarely dwelt in its precincts, and yet a few years
of rest would usually suffice to heal the wounds
inflicted upon it, and to restore this fertile oasis to its
former splendour.

"Herat possesses, in fact, the main requisites for
a flourishing agriculture. The climate is temperate,
and the hottest days are followed by cool evenings

and refreshing dews. Of water, that most essential element, there is abundance. There are, first of all, the two principal rivers, the Murghab and the Heri-Rud, both of which run in a north-western direction towards the Turkoman steppe, and absorb in their onward course a considerable number of smaller streams and rivulets. The Tinghilab and the Keshef-rud empty into the Heri-Rud, which flows along the Persian frontier; the Kolari and the Khushk empty into the Murghab, the latter river having for its tributaries the Magor and the Kizil-Bulak, besides many brooks. Such a great abundance of water, within a territory relatively small, cannot be met with anywhere in Central Asia, Persia, Turkey, and Arabia; and any one, familiar with the important part assigned to water by the Asiatic, will not be surprised at all to learn that Herat has always been deemed a jewel, the possession of which has been coveted by every conqueror, and, as experience teaches, continues to be coveted to this day. And, indeed, to this very wealth of Herat we must look for an explanation of the fact that the conquerors, for the time being, have succeeded in maintaining their ascendancy only so long as they were able to impress the governors appointed by them with a sense of their power. For, no sooner had the central power relaxed, when the governors were enabled to extract, from the ample revenues of the province, sufficient means to conquer their independence. This has been the case at all times ; and, referring only to the most recent past, I will mention that neither Teheran, nor Ispahan, nor Kabul, were able to maintain the sovereign rights of the crown in Herat for any length of time. In this way was Shah Kamram, Yar Mohammed Khan, enabled to successfully resist, during the years following 1840, the Barekzis; and after 1860 a similar success was vouchsafed to the efforts made in that direction by the then ruler, Sultan Ahmed. Nay, we had the self-same experience, at quite a recent date, in the case of Ayoob Khan; and it very nearly came to pass that Khuddus Khan himself, the appointee of the present Emir of Afghanistan, seized the reins of government, and made Herat independent of Kabul.

"The fact that Herat has, at all times, defied the sovereign rights of its rulers, must not be ascribed to its being remote from the centre of power, but to the wealth of its soil, which not only sufficed to amply meet the expenses of the administration, but furnished, besides, means for adventurous enterprises.

"I shall not attempt to state the income of Herat in figures, for in the entire absence of statistical data to that effect, any such statement would be only illusory; but, on the strength of my personal observa-

tions, I feel justified in assuring those who are present that, under a European administration, Herat
might develop into a veritable gold mine, meeting
not only the expenses of a costly administration, but
admitting of the most generous investments in the
future.   Especially now that the great curse of the
land, the so-called Khouf-i-Turkmen—that is, the
dread of the Turkomans—has been removed, and the
ravaging flood of the marauding incursions from the
north has been dammed up by the position of Russia,
a state of things may be brought about in that district such as has never been witnessed or experienced
there before.   The Badghis, more particularly, which
has been so well described by the masterly pen of Sir
Henry Rawlinson in the April number of the "Nineteenth Century," 1885, has now a chance of flourishing
anew, and rendering Herat, in good truth, the
granary of Central Asia. The fields, which were
lying fallow until now, will be resplendent with luxuriant vegetation ; and I do not exaggerate in asserting
that Herat may become a source of revenue ten
times as large as it has hitherto been.

"You will, therefore, perceive, gentlemen, the importance of Herat from an economic point of view.   I
shall now address myself to its ethnical conditions,
and may remark, in particular, in this connection,
that the various populations collected and settled here,

in the course of history, furnish the best means for
the conqueror to gain a foothold there, and to found
his rule on the firmest basis imaginable. Whilst, on
the one hand, the compact mass of Turkeydom is
found in the north of the Paropamisus, extending
far beyond the right bank of the Oxus, the bulk of
Afghan elements in the south, and the unalloyed
Irandom is predominating in the west, Herat is
inhabited, on the other hand, by ethnical fragments,
whose separate interests, national and religious, render
a home government impossible, to the same extent
that they increase and support the chances of a
foreign rule. The aboriginal population is, as is well
known, Iranian, and has always been distinguished
for its disposition to culture, its peaceableness, its
repugnance against military service, and thorough
devotion to the Government of the land. To this
race belong the Sunnite and Shiite Persians of Herat,
the Parsivans, properly Pars Zeban, meaning Persian-
speaking, to the south, as far as Sebzevar and Ferrah,
people who are physically classed as East Iranians,
and whose wit and civilisation have always struck me
as much as those of the modern man of Ispahan or
Shirar. From amongst them have arisen the great
minds of Moslem learning in the fifteenth and sixteenth centuries, for the long list of Herat celebrities,
glorified by Baber in his memoirs, belongs for the

most part to that race. They have always formed the
cream of society, but in war and politics they were
ever the hindmost, and willing to accept, without
reluctance, any foreign rule that happened to prevail,
for the time being. The rest of the population is
comprehended under the common appellation of the
Tchihar-Aimak, that is, four tribes, a politico-ethnical
expression, dating from the time of the Timurides,
and by which those entirely strange elements were
designated, who had been assisting the hosts of the
Timurides, in their wars against their western and
southern neighbours. Regarding the number of these
Tchihar-Aimaks, I could glean but little that was
positive, nor am I disposed to have much faith in the
reliability of the statements made in that direction
by the latest informant, the correspondent of *The
Times* with the Afghan Frontier Commission. The
Jemshidis on the Khushk and along the Murghab river, are said to have numbered, two centuries
ago, as many as sixty thousand families, and are now
reduced to not quite six thousand families. The
Firuzkuhis, their neighbours to the east, having
Kalei-Nau (New Fort) for their centre, number eleven
thousand families. Both are of unmixed Iranian
origin, and belong to that fraction of their race,
which in remote antiquity already had settled in the
mountains, along the border of the Iranian element,

as a sentinel post, for which reason they obtained the collective name of Galtcha, a name which is now applied to the Persian mountaineers in the neighbourhood of Samarkand.   Even fewer particulars are known about the Teimenis, who are living in the south, and are, for the most part, farmers and tradesmen; and about the Timuris we know no more than that they are occupying the border regions between Persia and Herat, and are tributaries, now of one, now of the other.   The number of the entire population of Herat may be computed to exceed one million—a million of a race physically and mentally strong, divided, as I said before, amongst themselves by antagonistic interests, noted for their common hate and detestation of the Afghans as well as the Persians, and whose loftiest ideal has always been the independence of Herat.   This ideal, however, Herat has been able to grasp until now but rarely, and that only for a very short space of time; but the course of historical events is undergoing a great change in Asia.   Herat is standing on the threshold of an extraordinary metamorphosis, and whichever of the two European rivals may chance to get possession of it, he will be sure to avail himself of the favourable circumstances to obtain a firm hold there, and will find an essential support in the above-mentioned Tchihar-Aimaks.   The Firuzkuhis, Jemshidis, and

Timuris, reared as they are in warfare, may be trans-
formed, at but a small expense, into an excellent
militia, and trained into becoming a reliable barrier
against Afghanistan and Persia, in the defence of the
borders of the country, whilst, at the same time, under
the protection of a stable Government the Parsivans
and Tadjiks may develop into becoming powerful
agencies of commerce and industry.

"The situation of Herat is, in fact, such an one that,
in its commercial and strategic importance, it is surpassed by but few cities in Asia. The commerce of
India, Sogdia, and China reached the west in ancient
times by passing through Herat, along the north of
Persia, and through the Caucasus, and continued to
follow that route until the incursion of the Mongols,
and to some extent even up to a later time. Even
during our own century—nay, until quite recently—
Herat has been the emporium for tea and indigo, on
the one hand, and American and English wares, such
as cotton fabrics, cloth, trinkets, etc., on the other
hand. I myself have witnessed the unpacking of,
and trading in, the various articles at the numerous
caravansaries, and so extensive had the trade between
the north and south become, that the villagers in the
near vicinity of Herat earned, for the most part, their
livelihood by the business of transportation. At the
time I was there, there were in Kerrukh alone eight

wealthy Kervanbashis, who managed with their numerous camels the transportation between Meshed, Bokhara, and Kandahar. The merchant from Lohani and Kabul most likely conveyed his own caravans to Herat, but the merchants of Bokhara and Meshed were compelled to employ the Herat forwarders; and that Herat had always served as a channel of communication between the north, south, and west, is proved by the description given by the historians of the past of the splendour of its bazaars, of which, it is true, there now remain but miserable ruins.

" Nature and man have co-operated in establishing the importance of this place. You are well aware of the fact, gentlemen, that all the conquerors of India of bygone days have passed through Herat, have marshalled their armies there, and allowed them to rest at Herat in order to prepare them for the change of temperature in the southern latitudes. To this very day, this traditional highway to India is preferred to the route over the Hindoo Koosh and Kabul, not only by armies and caravans, but by solitary travellers, such as the pilgrims to Mecca. The pilgrim allows three months for his journey from Herat to Karachi—a long stretch of road, frequently deficient in water; and yet he prefers it to the mountain road running more to the east, a road which, of all the conquerors of India, was attempted only by

Baber and his courageous companions in arms. I wish to call your attention to the additional circumstance that almost every conqueror of India, advancing from the north to the south, had secured the possession of Merv, and of the oasis on the lower course of the Murghab, before he proceeded to attack Herat. Timur did not invest the city on the Heri-Rud until he had reduced the Turkomans about Merv, and placed them under his banners. The same thing was done by Sheibani, the prince of the Uzbegs, in the beginning of the sixteenth century, when he first took Merv, and subsequently Herat. Nadir Shah, too, has proceeded in the same manner; and it is quite remarkable that Russia, which is also advancing from the north to the south, is pursuing the identical policy, planting her banner on the ruins of Merv, after having subjected the three Turkestan khanates and reduced the Turkomans; and, in order to be quite consistent in acting up to the example set by a Timur and a Sheibani, she now approaches the frontiers of Herat, with the view, as may be imagined, of obtaining possession of the city on the Heri-Rud, and getting into her hands the important central point which is indispensable to the further pursuit of her ulterior plans.

"But as this event has been instrumental in bringing about the recent conflict between England and

ɪ 2

Russia, and I am fully determined not to discuss politics in this hall, I shall abstain from speaking here about Russian claims to Penjdeh, and the intended frontier line from the Zulfikar Pass over Akrobat, extending south of Penjdeh. I shall instead advert to the fact that, as far as historical memory goes back, the district of Badghis has always formed a component part of the province of Herat, and was not, at any time, presumed to be a part of either Merv, Meshed, or Nishapur respectively. Even during the period of the splendour of Herat, under Sharukh Mirza and Hussein Mirza, Badghis had a governor of its own, entirely independent of Merv and Meshed; and the same was the case under the Sevfides, who, as is known, followed the Timurides and the Uzbegs in their rule. The conditions of such a frontier lie in the nature of things, for there, where the Badghis ceases, begin the sand regions of the Turkoman steppe. Nature herself has drawn here the precise line of demarcation, and Penjdeh, as well as Akrobat, being situated within the lines of the cultivated soil of the north-western offshoots of the Paropamisus, they belong to Badghis, and are part of the district of Herat—such parts as are, so to say, the keys of the routes along which the main highway can be reached without any trouble. The acquisition of Herat is only a question of time—

and that of a very short time—with the Power that happens to get hold of the said points, for, considering the disfavour with which the Tchihar-Aimaks and the Hezares are viewing the Afghan *régime*, it will be an easy matter for a well-regulated European Power to conciliate the sympathy of these populations, and, sustained by their goodwill, to obtain possession of Herat."

CHAPTER VIII.

HAVING demonstrated the importance of Herat as a starting-point for armies, caravans—nay, for single travellers, on a march towards India, I may now proceed to sketch briefly the chances Russia enjoys for her future schemes upon that town, supposing, as I do, that nobody expects her remaining in Penjdeh or in Pul-i-Khatun, and that these two points will form but the last station of her advance towards the south.

But, first of all, we must point to the facilities Russia will acquire through her immediate neighbourhood with the Tchihar-Aimaks, tribes living under the unsettled rule of the Afghans, and who, even with the most peaceful dispositions, can hardly avoid becoming causes of frontier troubles and sundry dissensions. The Russians, located at Penjdeh, and taking particular care of their Sarik subjects, will very soon find fault either with the Jemshidis on the Khushk, or with the Hezares and

Firuzkuhis, on the Upper Murghab. Of the lurking hostilities between the Afghans and Russians, with whom the catastrophe of the 30th of March will always remain fresh in memory, I will not speak at all, being almost sure that the variance subsisting between these two new neighbours can hardly disappear without a fresh act of revenge. Add to this the boundless ambition of the Russian officers at the frontier: their insatiable lust for decorations and promotions, and above all, the long-ago settled line of policy to take Herat, whatever may be the assurances of the Czar to the contrary; and we may be fully convinced that the dormant desire for the possession of that city will not remain long unfulfilled.

It has been made lately the subject of special speculation of English political writers that the Court of St. Petersburg, in order to disguise its real line of policy, means either to hand over that town to the Persians, or by using Ayoob Khan, the most formidable rival of Abdurrahman Khan, as a puppet in his place, will reserve this *protégé* of hers for her future schemes. I believe none of these suppositions to be well-founded; for, admitting that Ayoob Khan's imprisonment in Teheran be only a respectful detention, and that he is very likely to be let loose on the outbreak of serious complications, I

still firmly believe that Russia will never trust any
allies or puppets, but that she will take the place
into her own hands, will fortify it, and, by connecting
it with the railway running from Sarakhs along the
Heri-Rud, will succeed in making of the ancient
capital of Khorassan the commercial centre and
place d'armes this town has at all times been, and
is capable of being in the future. In fact, what
Tiflis has become to the Caucasus, Herat will become
to eastern Khorassan; and, I may add, in a comparatively shorter time, and with much greater
facilities, for there are no troublesome warlike
ethnical elements to be conquered and to be kept
down, such as were the Circassians, Tchetchentzians,
Lezghians, etc. In Herat no Sheikh Shamil can
come forward to unfurl the banner of holy war,
and to wage a protracted struggle against Russia.

It has been generally overlooked that, with the
possession of Herat, Russia will get an undisputed
sway over the whole country stretching in the north
towards the Oxus; I mean not only over Maimene
and Andkhoi, but also over Kunduz, Aktche, Serpul,
and Shiburgan—nay, over the whole of Afghan
Turkestan, where the entire structure of Afghan
power rests upon rotten foundations, and may be
at any moment overthrown. I do not allude to the
dubious condition of fidelity and allegiance of Ishak

Khan, the Governor of Balkh, the dear cousin of the present ruler of Kabul, who behaves like a semi-independent prince, and has looked for a long time with longing eyes towards Tashkend; but I allude to the ethnical and political condition of this country on the left bank of the Oxus, such an one as greatly favours Russian intentions in a district which has been constantly undermined during the last years. As to the political claims, we have had many opportunities of seeing how Russian newspaper-writers, travellers—nay, statesmen and military authorities, were zealous to vindicate the right of the Emir of Bokhara to these countries, a right which is historically well founded; for beginning with the appearance of the Turk on the scene of events up to recent times, the small aforesaid khanates, including Andkhoi and Maimene, have been really governed from the banks of the Zerefshan, and have been regarded as dependencies of the khanate of Bokhara. Concerning the ethnical conditions, we must point out that the preponderating majority of the inhabitants are Turks. The Ersari Turkomans, mixed with other clans of the same nationality, are living on the left banks of the Oxus, from Tchardjui, beyond Kodja-Salih, whilst the Achmayli in Serpul, the Ming and Daz in Maimene, the Kungrat in Aktche, the Kiptchaks in the environs of Balkh, the Kangli in Khulm, and a mixture of Afshars and Kara-Turkomans in Andkhoi, may be said to amount to an average number of one million.

Now, these Turks have ever been the most bitter enemies of the Afghans, in whom they found not only a national aversion, but also the most reckless tyranny, for the rapacious and plundering propensities of the Afghan officials are able to alienate the sympathies and good-will of the most patient of subjects. Whilst living amongst these Turks I had plenty of opportunity to convince myself of the wretched condition the people were living in; the meaning of the proverb, *Hilmi Uzbeg Zulmi Awghan—i.e*, Uzbeg mildness and Afghan tyranny—became clear to me; and I was not in the least astonished when Colonel Grodckoff, travelling years later in those districts, made similar remarks, and heard similar complaints of the Turks groaning under the Afghan yoke. Of course, merciful Russia did not neglect to impart to these poor victims the idea of humanity and blessing with which the rule of the White Padishah is connected. All the Russian travellers in that part have strengthened them in that belief; and Russia, once in possession of Herat, is almost sure to avail herself of the sympathies thus artificially produced.

Last, but not least, we may mention the commercial advantages to Russia, which may prove a very solid bond in fastening the newly acquired Herat to the bulk of her possessions in Asia. Attentive travellers may have noticed, for nearly two decades back, the slowly but steadily advancing tide of Russian imports from the southern shore of the Caspian sea, through Mazendran and Khorassan. The beginning was made by the trading company Kavkaz-i-Merkur, richly subsidised by the Government, the agents of which were spreading all over eastern Persia; and whilst I was travelling in the country the bazaars of Shahrud, Nishapur, Meshed, and even of Herat were glutted with Russian wares. Quite recently sugar, chintzes, iron ware, arms, trinkets, etc., almost exclusively of Russian make, are to be met with along the whole line; and if we consider the extraordinary facility of communication produced, partly by the railway laid down in Transcaspia, partly by the opening of the road between Bokhara, Merv, and Sarakhs, we may well anticipate the unusual development which the Russian trade, coming in two different channels, will and must take in the north of Afghanistan and Persia, and that any effort of the English to outrival the competition will be vain and hopeless.

CHAPTER IX.

Now that the worst has befallen, and England, apparently, is compelled to become resigned to her fate, the question forces itself upon us whether Russia shall be allowed to go on as hitherto, encouraged by the ominous acquiescence and criminal indifference of English statesmen, in her usual way of aggression, or whether an entire change of British policy in Central Asia has not become an imperative necessity? I suppose that every sober-minded and patriotic Englishman will agree with me when I say that, considering the imminent danger lurking in every movement springing from indecision and an effete policy, the statesmen of Great Britain must make up their minds to look coming events boldly in the face. They can recede no more—not even a single step; and asserting the fearlessness common to the English character, they must declare to Russia : So far you have come, but further you shall not come; the time for subterfuges and empty diplomatising is gone by,

and every future move towards the south will be
looked upon as a declaration of war against England,
and will be opposed with all the available power
of Great Britain and India.   And, indeed, only the
intentionally blind will still doubt the approaching danger.   The famous saying of Mr. Gladstone
(*vide* his speech, November 27, 1878): "I have no
fear myself of the territorial extensions of Russia—no
fear of them whatever; I think such fears are only
old woman's fears," can hardly find its supporters
nowadays.   The Duke of Argyll wrote a very few
years ago: "My own view has always been that the
conquest by Russia of the Tekke-Turkomans and of
all the tribes of Central Asia has been inevitable.   I
have held, further, that no civilisation and no commerce could be established in those regions until that
conquest had been accomplished, and that on this
ground, as well as on several other grounds, it was at
once useless and undignified on our part to be per-
petually remonstrating against 'advances' which we
could not prevent, and which, in the interests of
humanity, we ought not to regret."   I daresay that
illustrious statesman will consider twice before he
utters such a view, concerning the Russian conquest
of Herat.

Henceforward all parties in England must agree
that Russia's hostile designs against India are patent;

that all the humanitarian and civilising work, with which Russia has been making pretence hitherto, is a mere humbug, and that all hopes for a mutual understanding in the future—I mean the division of the Asiatic spoil, of which we shall speak hereafter—are null and void. It is, at all events, a most saddening spectacle that Russia, led on and encouraged by English self-delusion, has succeeded hitherto in securing material and enormous advantages over her rival; such advantages as will form a standing peril to England, and will hardly be overcome, not even by the most extraordinary pluck and perseverance, which are the pre-eminent qualities of the Anglo-Saxon race.

First of all, we may hint at the uninterrupted chain of communication Russia has in her rear, from the interior of the mother country to the very gate of India. It is abundantly known that, besides the Caucasus having a standing army of from 120,000 to 150,000 men, Russia is able to get support from Odessa to Batoum in one day; from Batoum to Baku a train is able to run in eighteen hours, and from the last-named place, across the Caspian sea, steamers run to Mikhailofsk in twenty-four hours. Here begins the Transcaspian Railway—it will soon be finished to Ashkabad—the prolongation of which has been recently sanctioned as far as Sarakhs, enabling Russia thus to send troops in something less than six days from Odessa to Sarakhs, which is a hundred miles distant from Herat; whilst the English, supposing the railway sanctioned by the Government as far as Pishin to be finished in two years, are still 470 miles distant from Herat. We may add as well, that the one hundred miles separating Russia from Herat lie in a fertile, level and well watered country, whilst the 470 miles an English army would have to make, pass through a frequently arid tract, and haunted by a population, the friendly feelings and assistance of which cannot always be relied upon. In summing up briefly what we said before, we can state that Russia will be able to march to Herat from her railway terminus in eight or ten days, whilst England, considering the great distance, would require forty-seven days; to say the least an extraordinary difference in time and in the facilities of locomotion, if we consider the important part railways are playing in modern warfare.

Reflecting, therefore, upon this great drawback England has to contend with in any future complications with Russia, which through her position in Penjdeh has become an imminent threat, it would be the most perilous self-delusion to adhere in future to the principle of Afghan neutrality, or of Afghan friendship; a principle laid down by such statesmen only as, eager to shirk liabilities and fond of patchwork, were either short-sighted enough to ignore unmistakable facts, or betrayed utter want of patriotism in trying to put on the shoulders of their successors burdens such as they themselves did not feel equal to sustaining. I have always ridiculed the idea of making a buffer of the country of the Afghans, being fully convinced of the want of elasticity of the material employed for that purpose. I never was a believer in Afghan friendship, and even now I believe that such sympathies will come forward only if far greater dangers threatening from the north compel the unruly fanatic mountaineers beyond the Suleiman range to look to the British lion for shelter. In the meantime I should not wait until the whole nation gets convinced of the necessity of such a step. But the idea of a whole Afghan nation being a preposterous one, considering that these unmanageable elements can be hardly ever roused into unity, it suggests itself to now make use of that portion of the national element which stands nearest to the possibility of a voluntary movement of that character; that portion which is headed now by a prince aware of the gravity of the situation, and who, owing to his thorough knowledge of the character of greedy, faithless, and despotic Russia, will give preference to English offers of amity, and who, utterly convinced of the necessity of yielding, will and must prefer to lose one portion of his dominions rather than to risk the whole, and to stake his crown and the independence of his nation.

I am fully aware of the great aversion felt in England, particularly by a certain party in the country, to any policy which would involve fresh hostilities against Afghanistan, *i.e.*, a third Afghan war. Well: if there is any possibility of a reasonable reliance upon the good faith of Emir Abdurrahman, of course it would be better to avoid any coërcive measure causing war, and to convince that ruler that it is his own interest to have the railway extended from the Indus up to Kandahar, with a telegraph line as far as Herat. For the sake of not giving umbrage to the suspicious Afghans, I would agree with the military correspondent of *The Times* (May 26) to have the terminus of the railway outside Kandahar held eventually by a small picked garrison of 200 or 300 native troops. But, as to Herat, I believe that there cannot be any consideration for Afghan susceptibilities; as the fortifications of that place must be put in a proper state of defence at British cost and superintended by officers of the Royal Engineers. The escort of the resident should consist of a regiment of sepoys, of a company of pioneers, of a squadron of native cavalry, and of a battery of native artillery; and provisioned for six months, as the above-

J

quoted military correspondent suggests it could be if lodged in the citadel, this would be the best safeguard against a Russian *coup de main*, which has become recently, since the occupation of Penjdeh, such an imminent danger.

Now, to such propositions people will naturally object by saying: We won't jeopardise the lives of our officers at the distant outposts, we will have no renewal of catastrophes like those of Burnes and Cavagnari in Kabul, and we abhor any transaction based upon the amity of the Afghans. My answer to such objections is simply this, that if the Emir is unwilling or incapable to afford sufficient protection to those who labour for the safety of his crown and national independence, then he is either not the *de facto* ruler of his country, or he harbours hostile feelings against England; and in either case, England must resort to force, and carry out the measures of defence of her own frontiers with every means at her disposal. This would, of course, mean a third Afghan war, a shocking eventuality for many English politicians: but since Russia cannot and ought not to be permitted to occupy at random this important place, which would make her, practically, master of all Afghanistan, and ruin for ever British *prestige* in Asia, I believe that of the two evils, namely, a war with Russia or Afghanistan, the lesser one must

be chosen, for there can be no mistake about it
that the immediate neighbourhood of Russia to India
is far more dangerous, and may prove far more costly
than any forcible seizure of Kandahar, or garrisoning
of Herat. If the Liberals had not pursued the
suicidal policy of evacuating Kandahar in 1880, a blun-
der which they themselves now regretfully acknow-
ledge, as I myself had occasion to hear during my
last stay in England from the lips of eminent Liberal
statesmen, the eventuality of a third Afghan war
would be entirely beyond the range of any possibility.
But this national calamity cannot be now repaired,
and if Emir Abdurrahman, who was invited, a poor
beggar, to sit on the throne of his cousin, and would
have been ready to concede at that time any condition offered, be likely now to oppose, and even to
fight against the execution of these schemes, salutary
to himself and to the interest of Great Britain, I
beg leave to remark that even in that case England
ought not to retreat from carrying out the unavoidable measures for the defence of her frontier. As
matters stand to-day, the Emir will certainly consider
twice of it before he enters into hostilities with
England, and I am not in the least afraid of his
making common cause with Russia and in casting his
lot with the conqueror of the north. The disastrous
fate which has befallen his uncle, Shir Ali Khan,

J 2

rises up before his vision like a dread spectre. A
twelve years' intimate connection with Russian officers
has fully imparted to him the knowledge of the
faithlessness and unreliableness of the Muscovites;
and really, if such had not been the case, he would
have long ago been caught in the net of Russian intrigues, and beguiled by promises profusely sent
from Tashkend, would not have come to Rawul
Pindi, and would not have fought Alikhanoff on the
Khushk. As to the people of Kandahar, there is
not the slightest apprehension of their resistance, as
we formerly stated. The west of Afghanistan is
quite different from the east and north of that
country. Here the Afghan element is not so compact, for it reaches only to the Hilmend, or, at the
utmost, beyond Girishk, nor is it conspicuous for those
military qualities generally applied to the whole
nation.

Sir Richard Temple, who speaks of the Afghans
as a fighting race, and who gives full credit to their
martial virtues, says, among other things: "This
description is applicable fully to the country around
Kabul, and to northern Afghanistan, but in a much
less degree to the country round Kandahar, and to
southern Afghanistan; indeed, many believe that the
city and district of Kandahar could, if necessary, be
permanently held. There is a considerable difference

between the character of the northern tribes and that
of the southern."

In summing up, therefore, all the means of defence available to England, we must come to the
conclusion that the line of policy hitherto followed,
with regard to Afghanistan, must undergo an entire
and radical change. The time for experimenting is
irrevocably gone; the idea of convincing the Emir of
British friendship, and getting in exchange for it
Afghan sympathies, must be dropped for ever, for should
he prove obstinately blind to his own interests, then
he cannot be used as an ally in the defence of India.
To dally with the sympathies of Asiatics, and particularly of Mohammedan Asiatics, is a pastime which only
Russia may permit herself, as she is quite superior to
England in duly appreciating the doubtful value of
such Eastern articles. She, above all, takes care to
fetter tightly her Asiatic neighbours or allies; she
even goes so far as to cripple them; and if these
allies or neighbours, after having been rendered
totally innocuous and powerless, will come forward
with their sympathies, she then only allows them to
make declarations of love, and only permits herself,
occasionally, the luxury of responding with a fond
simper. England, on the contrary, unable to understand the real value of Asiatic professions of amity,
has been too frequently misled in her dealings with

Mohammedan powers in Central Asia. She has opened her purse liberally, giving rich subsidies in money and in arms, forgetting entirely the lesson experience might have taught her, that this money and these arms will be employed by her good friends to fight her. What use is there in the £120,000 annually given to Emir Abdurrahman, refusing as he does, even now, to receive an English officer as an envoy and representative of the Viceroy? Whenever the attention of the Government has been called to this anomaly, we generally got to hear that the Emir could not guarantee the safety of the English representative against his fanatical and ill-disposed subjects. Is Sir Bartle Frere not quite right, when he remarks on this subject—"I have never believed in the validity of this objection, and I should consider it quite chimerical, unless it were formally stated by the Ruler himself. In that case, I should point out to him the absurdity of his calling himself the Ruler of a country where he could not ensure the safety of an honoured guest. I should decline to communicate with him except through a representative accredited to him like our envoys at other Asiatic courts, and I should state clearly the impossibility of our talking of friendly relations with a nation where our representative would not be welcomed." ("Afghanistan and South Africa," 5th edition, London, 1881, p. 36.)

So much for the main line of future Russian aggression through Afghanistan. As far as regards the lateral movements across the Oxus to Balkh, and over the Hindoo Koosh to Kabul, such movements are scarcely worth noticing, and the Russians were the first who, convinced of the impossibility of carrying out such a scheme, had years ago bestowed the greatest care upon the main road leading from the Caspian across the Turkoman country, through Herat. We have still further to allude to the way of communication, hitherto only secretly discussed, through the Pamir Plateau, which, starting from one of the passes of the Alai Mountains in Khokand, is said to convey a Russian column in a very short time to Yassin and Ghilghit, enabling the daring adventurers to drop down like a *Deus ex machinâ*, and to attack the English from a vulnerable and least expected side. As there is no historical record of such a feat in marching, we should rather turn our attention to a question which has in these latter days been the subject of so many and varied discussions—namely, to the military strength of the two rival Powers, and the skill and preparation necessitated by the future struggle. But this being the province of a strictly military pen, and being, therefore, utterly beyond the range of my literary powers, I beg to refer my reader to a chapter in Col. Malleson's lately published excellent little book, "The Russo-Afghan Question and the Invasion of India," headed "The Armies on both sides," an elaborate and exhaustive paper which affords us an insight into the military strength of both Powers available in a contest for India.

In connection with these statements I would only remark that, being accustomed to judge Russia, not from the extension she shows on the geographical maps, but from the strength she was able to display on the battlefields of Europe and Asia, I must say that I do not share the opinions of those who attribute to that gigantic empire such a formidable and extraordinary power of action. An army which ran a great risk of being thrown into the Danube, the Emperor and general staff included, by the ill-fed, half-naked, and emaciated Turkish soldiers, if the regiments of little Roumania had not hastened to her assistance—such an army I cannot call a formidable one. Still less does it inspire me with fear, if brought face to face with the hardy, plucky, and intrepid British soldiers of India, who, led by such generals as Donald Stewart, Roberts, Charles Macgregor, and others like them, would certainly keep up their old reputation, and do their duty for the welfare of the country. Why should we overlook the enormous difference existing between military material recruited from a free country, and led by highly-educated patriotic officers on the one hand, and between the poor slave forcibly enlisted by despotic power, and commanded by officers who, brought up in gambling, debauchery, and the indulgence in dissipations of every kind, can hardly be animated by the noble spirit of free men. Indeed, it is a bitter irony of fate to have to draw comparisons between the abilities of a nation standing at the top of our civilisation, the prototype of liberal institutions for the whole world, the luminous fountain of science and of many glorious achievements of mankind, and of a society noted for its abominable vices, where truth-speaking is an unheard-of occurrence, and where an emperor said "that he was only safe with his palace built of granite, which could not be stolen by his dear subjects or his surroundings."

In continuing to speak of the means of defence against Russian aggression upon India, we must at the same time remark that England should return to the position she occupied up to the last six years in the Mohammedan world at large, a position which she has forfeited through what can only be called the stupidity of a certain class of her statesmen, who, actuated by gross ignorance and mischievous party spirit, were foolish enough to sneer at those very conditions which gave strength to the English rule in India, and to English influence all over Moslem Asia. The reader

must know that, up to recent times, the Mohammedan
Asiatic conceived under the notion of Europe of two
main agencies.   One was the continually destructive,
encroaching, and extirpating power—namely, Russia
—whom he identified with Dedjal (the anti-Christ),
with the implacable enemy of Islam, who can never
be appeased, and with whom it is hopeless to make
any terms whatever.   As the second agency, and
quite in contrast to the former, he knew England,
whom he identified with the idea of Conservatism, of
peaceful and friendly neighbourhood, and in whom he
liked to discover a non-Mohammedan who could not
be styled a totally black unbeliever.   The English
Church has no images to worship, it does not admit
fanatic hatred of foreign religions, whilst the main
features of English character, such as coolness, com-
posure, steadiness, etc., are quite in keeping with
what a Turk, an Arab, and the rest of the Mohammedans, save the Persians, imagine under the name
of a gentleman.   During my long and intimate connection with Mohammedans in Asia, I always heard
them extolling the virtues of the English ; English
manufactures being the most solid, and the English
rule the most beneficent ; so that Central Asian
pilgrims, on starting from their distant homes,
through India to Mecca, were not half so afraid of
perils and hardships in store from them as those of

their colleagues whose way led them through Russia, and who brought back with them the most frightful accounts of the vexatious rapaciousness and cruelties they had been subjected to by the official and non-official world. In acquiring such experiences, I began to understand the secret of British supremacy in India, and I said to myself, what on earth could the English not achieve with this moral standing and reputation? The reader may imagine my astonishment, when I afterwards saw English statesmen priding themselves upon and glorying in the destruction of this eminent advantage, and, ridiculing what is called *prestige*, beginning to emulate Russia in her reckless and unjustifiable enmity against the Mohammedan world. I allude, of course, to the attitude assumed by the Liberal Ministry against Turkey, to the disgraceful comedy at Dulcigno, to the inglorious policy in Egypt, and to many, many other incidents aiming at the entire destruction of Turkey, of that only power in the world which can be of great service to England's standing in Asia, and cordial relations with which offer the best safeguard to English power in Mohammedan India.

Of course, there have been, and there are, even now, contradictory opinions as to the link existing between the Mohammedans of India and those of Turkey. I have read, quite recently, in a paper written by an evidently staunch Liberal, and published in the *Nineteenth Century* (April, 1885), the following remark:—"Judging from my own experience in India, I am of opinion that the vast majority of Mussulmans there, like the vast majority of Christians in Europe, are occupied chiefly with things of this world, taking thought for the morrow, how they may eat and drink, and wherewithal they may be clothed, and troubling their heads very little about the Caliph of Islam, his triumphs and defeats." Considering that this opinion is shared by many other influential statesmen of the same school, I beg leave to remark that " my own opinions," based upon a long and intimate connection with the Mohammedan world of Asia, have impressed me with the fact that there is a strong tie of unity between the true believers on the Indus and their co-religionaries on the Bosphorus; a unity which has manifested itself during the late Russo-Turkish war, through the large sums voluntarily contributed by Indian rice-merchants, landowners and Moulwis to the exchequer of Constantinople, and which can be easily fostered by the influential native press, and made a source of great discomfort to the English, should they persevere in their enmity towards the Caliph, the legally acknowledged head of the whole Mohammedan world. If the gentlemen in Downing Street are not aware of the fact that Hindoo Rajahs of Moslem faith, in returning from England, where they finished their studies, are most anxious to pay their respects to the Sultan at Stambul, I would gently whisper into their ear that there always are certain mollas, dervishes and sheiks, in the close proximity of the Sultan, who regularly undertake errands to Bombay, Calcutta, and Lahore, and who, returning from the distant East to the so-called *Hind Tekesi* (Indian Convent) in Constantinople, are generally the bearers of such messages and interchange of ideas, as fully testify to the common cause of the two extreme links of Moslem society.

The Sultan, although politically a sick and half-dead man, still represents, from a religious point of view, a great moral power; and as I remember well the words addressed by the late Reshid Pasha to a Hindoo Mohammedan of note in 1857, during the Sepoy mutiny—words which left a deep impression upon that fanatic man from the banks of the Indus, I may be well entitled to assume that words pronounced by the Sultan in a contrary meaning would not miss their effect. To Russia, Germany, Italy, etc., the Turk may be " unspeakable," and may be driven out "bag and baggage" from Europe; but to England's standing in Asia he may still be of great use, and an alliance with the Ottoman Empire

recommends itself best to ward off Russian encroachments in Asia.   Turkey, possessing even now 400,000
men of the best fighting material, is by no means
a contemptible ally, and will fill up the gap left
through the inefficiency of English military preparation.   With a comparatively small assistance of
money, England, without being compelled to use the
dubious blustering of the Germans, expressed in
the words : " Unser Volk in Waffen " (Our people
in arms), may soon get an army able to work
wonders in the interior of Asia, an army which will
certainly better answer expectations than the famous
united force of Europe sent against Russia during
the Crimean war, which force, directed by the intrigues of Napoleon III., made itself immortally
ridiculous by its achievements.

Persia, in every respect inferior to Turkey, and
unable therefore to offer similar advantages, can be
nevertheless of use to England, if the Shah can close
Khorassan against an invading Russian army ; if he
prohibits the carrying out of provisions beyond the
north-eastern frontier, and facilitates, at the same
time, the carrying into effect of English plans.   As to
those Mohammedans who now are under Russian rule
being brought into a connection with an eventual attempt to revolutionise the Bokharians, Khokandians,
and Khivans, I cannot agree with those English

politicians who put any faith in this ultimate measure. The flame of rebellion might be easily kindled by the adversary too, and in such a case England would fare worst, for Tadjiks, Sarts, and Uzbegs are cowards, and there is no power to rouse them against Russia, considering that the shadow of a Cossack suffices to strike terror into the breasts of hundreds of the settled inhabitants of the three khanates, who ought never to be compared with the Indian Mohammedan, the heir of the military virtues of his conquering ancestors.

It is only as to the Turkomans that I would make an exception, knowing them, as I do, from an intimate intercourse. These adventurous and unprincipled children of the desert, famous for their boundless greed, have been partly subdued by force of arms, and partly now adhere to Russia owing to the fact of the so-called "wandering rouble." But the rouble is a very poor champion if compared with the sovereign; its convincing power is certainly wanting in superiority, and English outbidding, properly applied, can easily bring Sariks, Salors, and Mervians, and, particularly, the Turkomans around Andkhoi, under the standard of England. For a transaction of this kind, England wants agents like Alikhanoff, Tahiroff, and Naziroff, who may be easily found in the ranks of the auxiliary Ottoman army, Osmanlis, whose language is understood by the Turkoman, and who, known as brothers, are able to turn the whole Turkoman nation into the camp of the English, if sufficiently assisted. As to the frequently discussed diversion against the Caucasus, the English may, by such a move, interrupt the despatch of military succour, but I do not believe in the possibility of revolutionising that country against Russia. The Georgian and Armenian nationalists, of whom we used to read in the English press, are in a minority hardly worth considering, and the only revolutionary element which might have created trouble, I mean the Mohammedan Circassians, have been long since driven out of the country by the sagacious and cautious Russians. Two-thirds of these warlike mountaineers, thus expatriated, have perished in Turkey.

In concluding this chapter, treating of the means of defence left to England, I cannot leave unmentioned one point, to which, though seemingly out of place from a foreigner, I nevertheless must allude as to the *fons et origo mali*. I mean, party politics in England, which have, of late, so essentially injured the Imperial interests of that country, and which really have done so much harm to England's position in Asia, that the most strenuous efforts of very many years to come may scarcely be able to heal the wounds and restore the respect and consideration for England, so wantonly destroyed by the selfishness of one party in its struggle against the other. The frivolity and short-sightedness exhibited by a certain political party, of late years, culminating in the famous Egyptian ophthalmy, was really of such a nature as to make people despair of the results of constitutional life. In a superficial judgment one might have taken the statesmen, who have been deliberately deceived by Russia step by step in Asia, who have made all Europe an enemy to England, and who have shown cold indifference whilst the *prestige* of Great Britain was going to pieces all over the world, either as miscreants, or as men escaped from the lunatic asylum. Foreigners, indeed, entertain such an opinion; but my experience has taught me that English statesmen, no matter to what party they belonged, were honest and patriotic in their intentions, and that it is only the great misfortune of the country that their political views are biassed by party spirit, employed even in cases where the actual merits of the respective measures are very questionable, and when it becomes patent that it is not the welfare of the country, but that of the party, which is aimed at.

In order to put an end, once for all, to the occurrence of such injurious eventualities, it seems to me

K

unavoidably necessary that, besides the two leading parties of the country, a third one, namely, a national and imperial party, should come forward —a party whose exclusive care should be bestowed upon the foreign relations of Great Britain, and who, alive to the importance of a great national policy befitting the vast dominions of the Queen-Empress, should not allow the honour of the country to drift at random through party strifes and rivalries.   But, where one party undoes the work achieved by its predecessors in power, the progress, nay, even the maintenance of imperial strength and power will become utterly impossible; and the worst of all is that, according to the Latin saying, " *inter duos litigantes tertius est gaudens,*" the *tertius*, namely, Russia, has really made the best out of these petty squabbles, and, whilst the English were quarrelling about the Why and How of the measures under consideration, the insidious bear was quietly trotting towards India.

CHAPTER X.

It is just the consideration of the above-quoted vacillation of the politicians of Great Britain, which reminds us of the extraordinary fact, that in default of a constantly and uniformly ruling spirit, England has been unable to decide to this day the question whether the possession of India ought to be defended by the seemingly natural barrier in the mountains of the north-west, involving the immediate neighbourhood of Russia on the Indus; or whether it would be more judicious to erect outworks, to have a *glâcis* of defence, and consequently not to allow the Cossack to approach either the Kheiber or the Bolan Passes. And strange to say, this highly serious and important question is even now left open for discussion in this country, called pre-eminently practical! *Hannibal ante portas*, and my English friends are continually quarrelling whether the Indus, the Hilmend, or the Heri-Rud ought to be made the line of defence! Certainly it is a most afflicting sight to see a man

K 2

who is attacked by a crafty enemy, pondering on the choice of arms at a moment when the hostile sword is at his throat.

It is not my intention to dwell here at any length on the views expressed by me with reference to this question, ten, fifteen, nay twenty years ago; for I suppose it is pretty well-known to the English reader, in general, that I always stood up in my writings for the erection of a bulwark for the defence of India which should be in due proportion to the object to be defended. I mean to say, I found it always evident—and I am glad to see myself sustained by the highest military authorities—that England absolutely needs outworks for a valid defence of her north-western frontier; that the idea of having Russia in the immediate neighbourhood of Hindostan must be definitely dropped, and nobody must dream any more of accepting the phrase an English statesman used to me twelve years ago :—"Just as I prefer having a well-dressed, educated and polite neighbour, instead of a dirty-looking savage barbarian, so we prefer having Russia close at our frontier, instead of the unruly, unmanageable, and wild Afghans." Nowadays everybody is convinced that India, under the present circumstances, is still to be compared to a powder-mill, into the vicinity of which no man of sound mind would admit an enemy, with burning tinder in his hand, ready to throw the incendiary spark into the powder of his neighbour, and anxious to turn to his advantage the ensuing explosion. Russia, indeed, has already tried, in 1878, to make such a stroke with her army collected on the Oxus, and she really planned what Skobeleff called :—"The means of a hard blow, struck in the front simultaneously with a mutiny fomented at the rear of the Indus." At that time the Congress of Berlin restrained the Russian arm ; nevertheless, it never ceased to be a favourite idea with her, carrying out the will of Skobeleff, who thus summed up this policy :—"It will be in the end our duty to organise masses of Asiatic cavalry, and to hurl them into India, under the banner of blood and pillage, as a vanguard, as it were, thus reviving the times of Tamerlane."

In considering the chance of Russian success in an attempt to foment a mutiny, and to cause a general or a partial rising, we must look solely to England's *present* situation in India, and, steadily keeping before our eyes the results of her policy so far, ask ourselves the pregnant question whether, during her rule of nearly a century, attended by the never-ceasing work of civilisation, she has so far succeeded in securing the sympathies of the 250,000,000 of foreign subjects under her sway, as to be justified in expecting that, at a critical moment, these subjects will not countenance a change of masters, and that they would look upon England's enemy as the enemy of India, and make common cause with her against any external attack.

The answer to this question is the pivot-point upon which the chances of the great contest between the two rival European colossi in Asia are turning; for England, even under most auspicious circumstances, strategically, would be hardly equal to the task of defending her gigantic empire against external attacks, if its inhabitants, averse to her sceptre, were to entertain at the same time, in hopes of bettering their fortunes, a secret longing for a new master. This question has been inquired into and discussed numberless times, in every imaginable aspect, within the last twenty years; nay, during the whole of this century; and if, in spite of the considerable literature which has sprung up in connection with it, I venture to say a word or two on the subject, I do so for the sole reason that, owing to the neutral stand-point I occupy, and to my experience, both practical and theoretical, amongst Asiatics, extending over a score of years, I consider myself qualified to treat it with the fullest objectivity. I repeat, with some emphasis, "amongst Asiatics," for it is in India that we find the richest fountain of Asiatic views of life, and hence have emanated all those peculiarities, prejudices, and superstitions, with which we constantly meet, in the shape of the most irreconcilable contrast with our own views of life, among the Turks, Arabs, Persians, Tartars, Afghans, etc., and which have occasioned such great difficulties in all efforts to diffuse the light of modern culture in the East. In India, where these contrasts make themselves oftener conspicuous, the work of transformation and modernisation has involved the greatest imaginable struggle ; and we have only to thank the tenacity of Englishmen, and the degree of high culture incident to British civilisation, that any breaches have been effected in these ancient ramparts of Asiatic effeteness, and, where the extreme points of the two civilisations so diametrically opposed to each other have come in contact, that there, in some places, the ideas of the nineteenth century have already begun to force their way.

Upon a closer examination of the gigantic work of the British civilisers, we find that of the two chief elements in India, the Brahminic and the Moslem, the former offers less resistance and proves much more amenable to civilising influence than the Mohammedan. In spite of the merciless rigour of the system of castes and the ritualistic laws, according to which no Vishnu-worshipper is permitted to come into direct contact with a Christian,

or even to allow the shadow of one to fall upon him,
the number of Hindostanees of Brahminic faith
educated in English schools and employed in the
British service by far exceeds the number of Moslem
Hindoos similarly educated and employed.   It would
be unjust to ascribe this ratio to the preponderating
majority of the Brahminic population, for the same
ratio is maintained in these districts even where the
Vishnu-worshippers happen to be in a minority. The
non-Mohammedan Hindoo represents, no doubt, the
primeval type of the Asiatic cast of mind, but the op-
pression he has been subjected to for over a thousand
years has rendered him more manageable and docile;
he submits with better grace to the dictates of the
foreign ruler than his Mohammedan countryman;
and if the latter has been lately complaining that he
is excluded from his share in the State offices, and is
less favoured by the English than his Hindoo neighbour, he may attribute the cause of this to himself.
For it was his Moslem fanaticism, coupled with the
recollection of the part he had once played as one of
the ruling class, which has always impeded, and, to
some extent, still renders impossible the work of
assimilation.

An attempt on the part of the English to cloak
over, or to ignore, this marked sullenness exhibited
by the Moslem element would be criminal, and would

terribly revenge itself in time. Let us own it frankly. Islam has manifested this feature in its struggle with occidental culture, in all the continent alike, throughout the whole length and breadth of its extent. Material decline may have made it susceptible to temporary impressions, but these impressions very soon glided off its body. It is, and remains, the old and incorrigible representative of Asiatic fanaticism, which will enter into no compromises with the modern march of the world, and will rather hasten towards sure and irretrievable ruin than yield to those ideas which the world of the unbelieving, the enemies of the Prophet, are proclaiming and propagating. I am by no means exaggerating when I assert, that, in the coalition of his fanatic brethren in faith, the Mohammedan in India stands foremost, and that the most stubborn opposition to the teachings of our civilisation will come from him. In doing so I am not guided quite by the views contained in a work of Mr. W. W. Hunter's, entitled *Our Indian Mussulmans*, and published many years ago, nor do I aim at that hot-bed of Vahabism in Patna, or the Zealotism of the Indian Moulwis, but I am speaking from my own personal experience, recalling my intimate intercourse with Indian Mohammedans of rank and position, in many lands of the Islam world, and especially calling to my mind the troops of half-naked,

savage-looking, and raving dervishes, all of them
Indians by birth, who are wildly rushing through
the countries of Islam, and appear, to their fellow-
believers of a foreign tongue, like some dread beings
engendered by intense religious mania.   I have
observed the same feature in princes and ex-princes
dressed after the European fashion and speaking
English fluently, who are living on the rich fees
obtained for their crowns, in pomp and high state on
the Thames, and are overwhelmed with marks of distinction by the Queen and the aristocracy of the land,
but who, although they make at times concessions to
European usages, are, nevertheless, inspired by the
wildest and most intense hatred of everything that is
Christian.

If, with a mind free from bias, we search for the
causes of this bitter hostility, we are unable to discover anything else but that animosity which always
exists between the ruled and the foreign rulers of a
country, particularly if they happen to be separated
by the wide gulf of differences in religion, funda-
mental differences in manners and views of life, and
more especially if Mohammedans and Christians are
the parties opposed to each other.   It would be hardly
possible to find any other important cause to account
for this unreasoning enmity—certainly not in the
changed circumstances of the Rajahs of to-day,

when compared ·with the situation of their predecessors, under their own native princes — not to
perceive which would be like simulating blindness.
Law, order, and perfect security, as we shall afterwards point out, have taken the place of Asiatic
absolutism and tyranny, and the insecurity of life
and property which formerly prevailed.

The improved situation in India, the blessings of
modern culture, the re-assertion of human rights, will
meet with appreciation and thanks here and there,
among the lowest classes of the people; but unfortunately in Asia, even more than in Europe, the
great masses are following their chosen leaders, either
religious or social; and as it is to these leaders
England has done most harm, the latter will not be
conciliated by concessions of any kind. It will take
a long time before people in Asia will become convinced of the errors of the old order of things, and
made to recognise the inhumanity and unnaturalness
of the oligarchy; and as England has borne down
most severely on this very oligarchy in the Moslem
portion of India, and, indeed, given it the death-blow,
one need not wonder if, in certain circles, at this early
day already, the advantage of Russian supremacy is
being talked about.

Whenever I have pressed these prominent and
cultivated Hindostanees, who were longing for a

change from English to Russian rule, as to the motives for their northern sympathies, I invariably got
the same answer :—" The Russians are more pliant,
they are less stiff in their intercourse ; their character,
their system of government, and their ideas in
general are more Asiatic than those of the English ;
they are much nearer to us, and, if fate has decreed a
foreign rule over us, we are likely to make better
arrangements with them than with the English."
We meet, at times, with similar voices in the
native press, especially the Moslem; and although
I am not disposed to immediately accept these utter-
ances as the universal expression of public opinion,
yet I deem the very existence of such arguments to
be of a critical nature, and am, therefore, far from
sharing the confidence prevailing in certain circles of
English politicians as regards the feelings of gratitude entertained by these adopted Asiatic children,
who have been reared with so much trouble and pains,
and at such an expense.

Leaving out of view the danger last adverted to,
there have been complaints latterly in the English
press about the excessive military power of the so-
called vassal States. These complaints are tolerably
well founded, for the 49,050,000 Mohammedans and
Hindoos living under the sway of native princes, who
have an army of 349,835 men and 4,327 cannon at

their disposal, will not be likely to be more sub-
servient to English interests in moments of danger
than the remaining 200,000,000 Asiatics who are the
absolute subjects of the English Crown, and may
cause serious troubles, in spite of the very questionable value of their military strength, brought lately
under notice by a paper of Sir Lepel Griffin. In this
connection the twenty-two Mohammedan vassal States
must be especially considered, and among them
Hyderabad, Bhopal, and Bhavalpur more particu-
cularly, owing to the not inconsiderable political
importance they can boast of. The first named, with
a population of 11,000,000, has 8,000 cavalry, 36,000
infantry, and 725 cannon; the second, with a population of not quite a million, has 2,200 foot-soldiers,
700 cavalry, and 60 cannon; whilst the third, although possessing a population of but half a million,
is maintaining, owing to her position as a border
State, even a much larger force. It is true that the
soldiers of these Mohammedan vassal States are far
behind the English in military training, but such a
lack might easily find a compensation in religious
fanaticism. A summons from one of those princes to
the entire Moslem world might be fraught with the
utmost danger to England, even without any instiga-
tion from abroad; and I am, therefore, altogether at
a loss to discover those elements of security which

would make the approach of the northern rival to the Indian frontier a matter of indifference to England; still less do I understand the ostentatious calmness paraded by certain political circles in England with regard to the possibility of such an event. Indeed, parading is the proper word to be used here; for the greatest optimist and Russophil must admit to himself the appropriateness in this case of the comparison, so frequently used, of the dynamite factory and the evil-minded neighbour, and concede the inevitable necessity of erecting an outwork in Afghanistan as the only strong and reliable barrier between the two rival Powers. That this is the real feeling in the matter is evident from the various measures adopted quite recently, initiated by those English politicians themselves who are trusting à *tout prix* to Russian friendship.

I am fully aware of the difference of opinion prevailing on this subject, a difference quite comprehensible, considering that the sympathies of the natives of India are generally judged from a point of view peculiar to the observer; and it is, therefore, necessary to quote on this subject a great Indian authority, an illustrious statesman and patriot—I mean the late Sir Bartle Frere—who speaks from personal observation. He says:—" But the danger [referring to a revolution in India] I apprehend

is not of this kind: it is twofold. First, there
is the danger which Dost Mohammed well described
to Burnes as like that apprehended when you see a
stranger looking over your garden wall; he may
be on his own side of the fence, and he may
make no seeming attempt to come over; but you
know he is there for no good, and you do your best
to dislodge him, and do not rest until you have
done so.

"If we suppose Afghanistan only so far Russianised that Russian travellers freely move about the
country, that Russian officers and men, not necessarily
in the pay of the Russian Government, but deserters,
possibly, or vagabonds from Russia, drill the Emir's
troops, cast his cannon, coin his rupees, and physic
him and his subjects, what would be the effect in
India? Can any man in his senses, who knows anything of India, doubt that the effect now, and for
many years to come, must be to disquiet every one in
India, except that great majority of the cultivators
who will go on cultivating without talking politics
till the crack of doom? Every Englishman, from
the Governor-General downwards, will be disquieted;
they will feel that a great foreign Power has as much
to say to the proceedings of all the troublesome
classes as the Viceroy and his English officials.
Every prince and chief will see in the Russians a

possible alternative claimant for empire in India ; all
the disaffected,' dangerous, and criminal classes will
be on the *qui vive,* ready to stir at a moment's notice ;
and all the millions who still have some martial
spirit left will furbish their swords, and believe that
another era of fighting and fair contest for martial
renown and plunder is at hand. All these elements
may be stirred into strife any moment by a Russian
proclamation issued at Kabul, or even by a false
report of one, for it is not necessary that the report
should be true to set some of these restless elements
in motion."

And that Russia will not be loth to avail herself
of this vulnerable point of her rival we must take for
granted. This *ultima ratio* is publicly spoken of
whenever the chances of the contest at issue are discussed. In order to give our readers an idea of
the language used on such occasions, we shall quote
the words of General Soboleff used in his incendiary
paper, published in the *Russ* last January. "England," says General Soboleff, the head of the Asiatic
department in St. Petersburg, a man whose enunciations weigh heavily in the scale of politics, "lays a
heavy hand on her dependent peoples ; she reduces
them to a state of slavery, only that English trade
may profit, and Englishmen grow rich. The death
of millions in India from starvation has been caused

indirectly by English despotism. And then the press of England disseminates far and wide the idea of Russia being a country of barbarians. Thousands of natives in India only await Russia's crusade of deliverance."

On reading words like these, and paying due consideration to the fact we have heretofore stated concerning the impossibility of admitting Russia close to India, we must dismiss, once for all, the idea of a co-terminous frontier on the Indus, as well as the frequently-ventilated plan of a peaceful and amicable division of the so-called Asiatic spoil between the two rival powers. Referring to the former, we must fully agree with Sir Richard Temple, who says :—" In other regions a boundary may be be fixed, on either side of which the two European empires in Asia may rest in peace and natural good-will. But that boundary must not be on the existing trans-Indus frontier of British India—that is, almost on the Indus itself. It would be impossible then for the two empires to co-exist in mutual trust and amity. Russia, indeed, might not be able to occupy Afghanistan in force ; such occupation might prove as arduous to her as it has proved to the English. But she might use diplomatic control or influence there right up to the mountain passes which are the gates of India, facing towards Central Asia. Such events

L

or circumstances would produce a profound impression on the vast population of British subjects of India, especially upon the educated classes, and also upon the native States. It has been shown how the spread of superior education is awakening the natives to an understanding of political affairs, and how important and numerous the native States really are. The effect not only of the proximity, but actually the contact, of such a power as Russia would be felt throughout the Indian Empire. Whether it would sap or undermine the loyalty of so many divers nationalities need not be discussed, but it would be indefinitely great beyond doubt. The imperial relations of England with India would then be very different from what they now are. One of the momentous consequences must be this: that England would have to maintain a much larger force of European troops in India than at present. If a considerable augmentation of the European garrison were to become necessary, then inevitably a large portion of the English army would be locked up in India. It is not necessary to dwell on the military difficulties that would arise, nor upon the financial embarrassments that would ensue."

With reference to the other idea, namely, the eventuality of a peaceful division of the spoils, an idea particularly cherished by those Continental

Powers in whose interest it lies to avert any complications which might possibly interfere with their
politics, and who care but very little for the welfare
of Great Britain, I need scarcely say that such an
idea is as foolish and egotistical as it is preposterous,
and scarcely worthy of consideration. To imagine
that ambitious Russia will pursue a policy, for
centuries, through the dreary steppes of Central
Asia, without any palpable results other than the
possession of the three khanates and of the Turkoman country—a possession which will never pay the
heavy sacrifices of blood and money—is really more
than political short-sightedness, for it is suggested by
intentional malice and black envy. Do people really
fancy, after Russia has spent over one hundred
millions of pounds during only the present century,
upon the carrying out of her old and favourite
scheme, that now she will stop, at the very gate
of India, and will resist all temptation coming
from the sunny land on the Ganges and on the
Indus? No, I cannot believe in the sincerity of
such an idea; its adoption would simply lull England into the sleep of false security, and encourage
Russia in her approach to the Achilles heel of her
rival. For whether Russia intends to solve the riddle
of the Eastern question by using the key to India in
order to open the gates of the Bosphorus, or whether

L 2

she covets the possession of rich India as an outlet to the southern seas, she, at all events, means mischief to England, mischief to the holy cause of our civilisation in the East, and mischief to the still more sacred interest of humanity at large.

CHAPTER XI.

HAVING spoken, hitherto, pre-eminently and exclusively to the English public, of the political rivalry
between England and Russia in Central Asia, I shall
now address myself to the European and American
readers interested in this question, trying to prove to
them that my sympathies with the cause of the
English do not rest simply on some unaccountable
freak; that I am not in love with one and hating the
other; but that the sympathies exhibited by me are
the outflowings of a long study, practical and theoretical, of a careful and impartial balancing of the
results these two representatives of our western
civilisation have been able to show hitherto in their
respective fields of activity. This comparative study
of English and Russian civilisations in the East, could
justly fill up a book by itself, and will cut a rather
sad figure in the narrow precincts of a single chapter;
but it is unavoidably necessary for me to hint at the

salient points of their divergency, flattering myself, as
do, with the hope that this Central Asian question,
slighted for so long a period by our diplomatists—
nay, even ridiculed by a certain class of politicians—
will not only interest England and Russia, but every
civilised community in the world. It is not a Central
Asiatic, but a strictly European question, of far-
reaching political and cultural importance.

Russia—so we read in the argumentations of
French and German political writers — being of
Asiatic origin, and conspicuous for many features
of Asiatic society, is far superior to England in propagating the doctrines and principles of our western
culture, and in introducing a settled rule and order
into the semi-barbarous countries of Asia, and more
fitted for that task than the stiff, rigidly cold, unpli-
able English.

In my controversies, covering nearly twenty years,
concerning this question, I have been often told, that
by overlooking the wide gulf which separated the
thoroughly Europeanised Englishmen from the
Asiatic, imbued with the spirit of the eastern culture,
thousands and thousands of years old, I generally
forget that a less refined agency, occupying the middle
position between the two opposed cultures, will and
can naturally serve as a more efficient intermediary, and
that, therefore, Russian society, standing as it were

on the verge of both cultural worlds, must decidedly prove a more successful propagator of our western lore in the East. Well, I never liked to be taken for a fanatic, nor did I ever indulge in obstinate negation; for I always admitted, and even now admit, that Russian civilisation, with all its drawbacks and vices, is still superior to that culture which is the offspring of Mohammedanism, and which, fruitful as the latter may have been in the past, is at present nothing but an abdication of the exertion of self-will, and a relapsing into the dark recesses of past ages. It would be a useless attempt to deny, that by introducing a settled rule into the formerly barbarous regions of Asia, where the reign of rapine and bloodshed has laid waste large tracts of country, Russia has conferred a good many blessings upon those miserable fellow-creatures of ours. But I beg leave to ask: can the state of things created through Russian agency, be really called civilisation, and does it represent even the faintest ray of that glorious light which we call the modern culture of the Christian West? And farther; who could find fault with us, if, knowing as we do of the existence of a purer channel, of a more enlightened torch-bearer, and anxious to give but the best to the poor oppressed Oriental, we should wish to substitute the more faithful representative of our ideas for the equivocal and unreliable Russian agent?

Facts being far more eloquent than theories, I shall pass in review before the reader those nationalities which have been undergoing for nearly four hundred years the Russian process of civilisation; and he will agree with me, that far from having gained anything, they are, at this day, losers morally and materially, and are as far from any notion of our western culture as any of their brethren living under fanatical Mohammedan rule.

Looking at the nearly half million of Kazan-Tartars, a mentally gifted fraction of the Turkish nation, and famous in olden times for its Moslem culture, we shall find that, excepting a few superficial features, such as the familiarity with modern European beverages, there is not the slightest trace of the world of the nineteenth century to be remarked in the social and political life of these stubborn Asiatics. If we except one or two Tartar books, containing very primitive instruction in geography, in the history of Russia, and translations of Russian fables, we may well contend that the Government has done nothing to raise the standard of education of these people; they are left in moral stupor, and all their mental discipline they owe to the schools established and sustained by themselves. There is in Kazan a public governmental school; but the tendency and spirit of the instruction are strictly Russian, and the effect counted upon is to turn the Tartars into Christians and Muscovites, in order that they may become much more easily engulfed into the already gigantic body of Muscovitism.

Of a similar nature will be our observations in viewing the condition of the Bashkirs, a likewise numerous fraction of the Turko-Tartar race, living in the Ural Mountains, who have inhabited this country from immemorial times, and who, in spite of having come nearly two centuries ago under Russian rule, are from a moral and material point of view still worse off than their brethren on the Volga. Poverty-stricken, neglected and derided by the fanatical ortho-dox Russian, their number has decreased nearly one-half from what it formerly has been. We might go on with observations of a like character, as far as Tobolsk in the north-east, and as far as the Altai Mountains in the south. We shall meet every-where with the fact, that at the appearance of the Russian coloniser the natives quickly disappear, and that the Government, instead of taking care of the cruelly oppressed subject, rather encourages the destructive work of the Russian Cossack, popa, and merchant.

In corroboration of our former statements, we shall let a Russian traveller speak for himself, by quoting the following passage from a paper published by M. Yadrintzeff, in the *Russische Revue :*—" The territory of the nomads is every day growing smaller, the Altais are being crowded out by Russiandom from their mountains, valleys, and forests, and the plain nomads and dwellers in the forest are being exploited in the most unscrupulous manner by the Russians, who employ for that purpose every species of cunning, cheating and violence. The Altai obtains for his native products, such as cedar-nuts, squirrel, and sable skins, cattle, etc., prices fixed for him by the Russian merchant himself, whilst he must pay for the products of Russian factories enormous prices, as for instance, for Arshin ladies' cloth, costing 60-70 kopeks, three roubles, and for chintzes, costing eighteen kopeks, forty kopeks. He is in addition, shamelessly taken advantage of by means of usury, and utterly ruined in health by the use of the deadly poison of *vodki,* so that the time is not very distant when the Turkish inhabitants of Siberia, totally impoverished and decimated by disease, will cease to have existed except in name."—

In view of this strong but truthful indictment, the charge of the famous General Soboleff: that England lays a heavy hand upon her peoples; that she reduces them to a state of slavery, *only that English trade may profit and Englishmen grow rich,* sounds rather curious, and the reader will find that I have been more than generous in calling the Russian efforts at civilisation in Asia a blessing to humanity.

Well; I am aware that the dear friends of Russia will always find one reason or another to exculpate the Muscovite civiliser. In this case, they will say that the failure cannot be ascribed to the want of ability of the ruler, but rather to the stubborn resistance Mohammedan society is offering almost everywhere to the civilising attempts of European conquerors; and they will quote amongst other things the Mohammedan of Algeria, and particularly the Moslem subjects of the Queen-Empress of India. As to the latter part of the comparison, we shall speak of it hereafter; but to prove the utter inefficiency of the civilising efforts of Russia, we must remark that she was as unsuccessful with those foreign national elements also under her rule, which have become Christians long ago, and who, belonging to the Greek orthodox faith, were entirely accessible to the civilising influence of the Russian Church and State. Let us take, as an example, the Tchuvashians, who live on the right bank of the Volga, and also on the left in a south-easterly direction as far as Orenburg, and have been since 1524 subjects of the Czar. This Turkish people, numbering nearly 600,000 souls, had embraced Christianity in 1743; they are continually and exclusively in the iron hands of the Russian administration, and have, in spite of being pre-eminently peaceful labourers of the soil, profited nothing by the advent of their new masters. The Tchuvashian is as ignorant and superstitious as before; he is only nominally a Christian, and secretly worships all the gods of his ancient pagan religion; a fact which may be useful to the ethnographer, but which is a standing shame to the success of the Russian civilisation which the friends of this northern power have lately trumpeted so much about in the world.

The state of the Ugrian population, such as the Tcheremissians, Votyaks, Ziryans, and Voguls, may be called a still more wretched one. Their daily life, their mode of thinking, and their social existence does not show the slightest influence of western civilisation; they have undergone little or no change since they came under the fatherly care of the Czar, whose Government, content to produce peaceful and willing taxpayers, thinks least of ameliorating the condition of the life of the people entrusted to its care. The result of this wanton neglect is quite naturally the gradual decrease of the conquered foreign elements, who are swallowed up by the bulk of Muscovitism, as we see in comparing statistical data of only half a century ago with those now extant. The Yakuts in the distant north, on the banks of the Lena, have dwindled down to nearly one-half of their

former number. The Voguls are almost on the point
of dying out altogether. The Krim-Tartars, a famous
conquering race, nearly half a million of souls up to
the beginning of the last century, have sunk to the
number of 80,000. The same appalling decrease in
numbers may be noticed in the Nogai-Tartars; the
renowned and independent mountaineers in the
western Caucasus have almost entirely disappeared;
and it is no exaggeration when we state that the
ethnographer, bent upon the description of the
foreign races subjected to Russia, must intone a dirge,
and look about for the spot where the people he
makes the object of his investigations have formerly
existed.

And how can it be otherwise, and how can we
expect from the Russian agency of civilisation any
better results? In accordance with the saying, that
the river cannot rise higher than the source, it would
be preposterous to expect from the Russian Government any degree of culture higher than she was able
to confer on her own subjects. A society where the
main principles of administration are wanting; where
bribery, embezzlement, and corruption are the order
of the day; and where every official, either civil or
military, is looking after his own personal interest,
and has not the faintest idea of duty, honesty, and
patriotism; there it is almost an impossible thing to

get the beneficent rule based upon right and legality, so indispensable to the welfare of the masses. " God is in Heaven and the Czar is far off in the north," exclaims the poor victim exposed to the unheard-of cruelty of Russian officials; his tears fall upon the ground and his woful eyes look to Heaven, but he peacefully and voluntarily submits, and is fleeced like a sheep. I could go on picturing the new state of things created by Russia in Central Asia, which has been made the subject of so many enconiums by her fanatic but utterly ignorant and stupid admirers. I could and will give on a future occasion extracts from letters which have reached me, coming from friends of mine in Central Asia, full of the most shocking details of Russian injustice and cruelty. But I suppose these few indications will suffice to convince the reader that there is much still left to be desired regarding Russian civilisation in Asia, and that we are quite justified in asking ourselves : Is this the noble light of culture, for the sake of which we should allow foreign nations to fall under the rule of Russia ? is this achievement a prize for which we ought to imperil the imperial power of a State like England, to whom all humanity is indebted for the most generous boons in the field of social and political work, and who has bestowed rare blessings upon the peoples entrusted to her care ?

I ask, above all, where is the European whose breast would not swell with pride at the glorious sight presented to the spectator in India, where a simple and unassuming trading Company began with securing a market for its trade, and finished by building up a gigantic empire of 1,500,000 square miles, with a population of nearly 250,000,000 ; an empire which surpasses in vastness and importance any colony founded, until now, by a conqueror under a foreign climate, and under such different social and political conditions; an empire where the united breaths of the conquered races would suffice to blow the small element representing the conquering race into the sea, yet where, nevertheless, the shadow of a single Briton suffices to overawe the vast multitudes, and to ensure obedience and respect for the doctrines of the civilisation imported from the distant West? I repeat that this aspect cannot leave the spectator of this extraordinary scene cold and indifferent; for he must find there the undeniable glorification of our western culture, the true success which has crowned the indomitable courage, the rare pluck and perseverance of the men brought up in the principles of the best light of modern civilisation; and ultimately he will perceive that liberal institutions, supported by a sense of justice and right, can thrive even on Asiatic soil.

If the high terms in which I speak of England's

doings in India should be taken for an outburst of
unconditional admiration, I will only point to the fact
that it is the ex-dervish, the ex-effendi, and the traveller amongst Eastern people as one of themselves, who
speaks in these lines ; it is the student of Eastern character, for years and years, who got the conviction that
it is easier to take a laden camel through a needle's eye,
than to penetrate the obstinately conservative mind of
an Oriental with anything like reform, innovation, and
new ideas.   If now I add that Hindostan is the cradle
and the fountain-head of all those qualities which constitute the true and unadulterated mode of Eastern
thinking, with all its queer notions of life, of politics,
and religion, my gentle reader will easily perceive the
utter astonishment I feel on seeing the success
English civilisers have obtained hitherto in that very
hot-bed of Asiaticism in India.   It is those only, in
fact, who have been eye-witnesses of the extraordinary
exertions and struggles which preceded even the
most insignificant reform in Turkey and in Persia;
only those who have seen how the good intentions of
the native rulers were shipwrecked on the immovable
rock of superstition, blind fatalism, and inveterate wil-
fulness ; who will be adequate to appreciate the work
done, up to this time, by the English.   I suppose I
am not expected to furnish here even an approximate
list of the respective details, for, what the bulky

volumes of H. S. Cunningham's "British India and its Rulers," or "Sir Richard Temple's "India in 1880," were able to give only in outline, though well defined, I could but with difficulty compress into the narrow limits of one chapter. I am only touching the main figures of this grand tableau, when I say that the spirit of our western civilisation is spreading like a spell over the vast tracts of this classic soil of Asiaticism, and the dawn of a new era can only remain unknown to those who, blinded by envy and intentional misconception, are eager to detect faults and shortcomings there, where splendid results have been patent and obvious.

We generally read on the Continent that these advantages of a better civilisation are dearly bought by the natives, at the price of extraordinarily heavy taxation; and cavillers go so far as to pretend that the *ryot* is more heavily burdened than any peasantry in Europe. To refute such an assertion, I will quote the very words which an Indian, not conspicuous for his English sympathies, said to me on this subject one day :—" In the time of our native rulers we could escape taxation through bribery and disorders in the administration, for several years' consecutively; we amassed a good amount of fat; but of what use was it? The Rajah, or any of his officials, suddenly swooped down upon us, and we had to pay not only

M

the fat, but sometimes also the skin, and the bones in
the bargain. Now we are very much like a milch-
cow; we are regularly fed by order, and justice introduced into the administration of the foreigners; but
we are also regularly milked by them, and the end of
it is that we save some fat, our skin and bones, and
on the whole, go on tolerably well."

Turning from the parable of this Oriental,
we may advert to official data, in quoting as to
the scale of existing taxation the following extract
from the report by the Famine Commission:—
"The general incidence of all taxation, including
the land revenue in this term, on the whole population is 4s. a head. The landed classes pay
about 5s. 6d. (44 annas) per head; but, excluding
the revenue they pay for their land to the State,
their share of taxation is 1s. 9d. (14 annas) per
head. The agricultural labourers pay taxes on their
liquor and salt, amounting to 1s. 8d. (or 13½ annas)
per head, or each family pays about a fortnight's
wages in the year. The artisans pay about 2s. (16
annas) each, or about the average earnings of five
working days. Traders pay 3s. 3d. (26 annas) each.
But any native of India who does not trade or own
land, and who chooses to drink no spirituous liquor
or to use no English cloth or iron, need pay in taxation only about 7d. a year on account of the salt he

consumes personally; and on a family of three persons the charge amounts to 1s. 9d., or about four days' wages of a labouring man and his wife."

Now, I would ask the bilious critics of Great Britain, whether the above-quoted taxation really be such a heavy price for the security which the natives of India enjoy; for the alleviation from the tyranny and despotism they had formerly to endure under the rule of their native princes; for the enlightenment they get in schools supported by the Government; for the vastly improved means of communication; and, in a word, for all the requirements of civilised life and modern progress? If wild detractors of England are indifferent to the fact that horrid crimes, such as the *Thagi*, consisting of way-laying and strangling travellers on lonely roadsides, and *Dacoity*, or gang-robbery, thriving formerly by reason of the fierceness and audacity of some classes, coupled with the timidity of others, have almost entirely disappeared, and that according to an Oriental saying, "A child can go on public roads carrying a basket full of gold on its head," owing to the safety produced by the police, I, for one, cannot share their indifference, remembering as I do the fear and anxiety travellers and caravans are exposed to in the different countries of Moham- medan Asia, nay, even in Russian Caucasia. It is the stern rule of the British which made the old crime of

Sati cease, whereby Hindoo widows were burned alive
on the funeral pyres of their husbands; and it is the
same rule which has done away with the shocking
female infanticides, by which hundreds of thousands
of poor innocent beings have been annually drowned
in the holy waters of the Ganges. It is owing to the
iron hand of British rule that rioting and disturbances arising from the hatred and fanaticism of the
various sects and creeds, that kidnapping, forgery,
adultery, and perjury are kept down, far better than
was formerly the case by the tenets of the religion of
the natives, and by the venal officers of the Rajahs.
The English law knows no difference between creeds
and colour, or caste and rank; and I can fairly imagine
the astonishment the Hindoo subjects of the Empress
must experience when the English tribunal gives
judgment in favour of the native, where an Englishman is the plaintiff, and when he finds that a verdict
is returned against even the Government itself; and
that of all places, in the East, where the proverb
exists: "In a lawsuit against the Padishah the
Prophet be thy lawyer."

Next to introducing order and security into social
and public life, the English Government have taken
particular care to ameliorate the condition of the agricultural class, and to raise the productiveness of the
soil. Asiatic countries depend, as is generally known,

on irrigation conducted from springs by ingenious contrivances, as a substitute for rain, the main source of fertility in temperate climates, but rare in the arid zones of the East. These irrigation canals constitute the real wealth and prosperity of Asiatic countries. In ancient times, the Eastern potentates were anxious to immortalise their names by creating such contrivances, but the rotten and decayed Mohammedan world has long since ceased to assist stepmotherly nature by digging canals. English rulers have therefore done a great work in reviving in India the times, past long ago, of the greatness of the native princes; they have partly restored the old existing irrigation canals, partly dug new ones, at considerable expense. To form an idea of the magnitude of the canal system of British India thus created, we may mention that the total length of the main canals and branches in the Presidences of Bengal, Madras and Bombay, amounts to 4,900 miles, of those of the Pendjab to 1,550, of Sind to 5,600, and in Northern India to 8,300; altogether to 20,350 miles, not including, however, the distributaries and other lesser canals not sufficiently known. The area now irrigated amounts to 1,000,000 acres in Madras and Bombay, 360,000 acres in Behar and Orissa, 1,450,000 acres in the north-western provinces, 1,350,000 acres in the Pendjab, and 1,250,000 acres in

Sind; in all 6,310,000 acres, or nearly six and a half millions of acres. The capital outlay by the State on this canal system may be set down about twenty and a quarter millions sterling, on which the net returns yield an interest of six per cent. (Sir Richard Temple, " India in 1880.")   In reading this account, we shall easily understand how India was able to send last year to England 10,000,000 cwt. of wheat, whereas ten years ago it sent only 1,000,000 ; an export sensibly felt in South Russia, Hungary, and all over Europe, but particularly in America ; an export which will presumably assume still larger dimensions, and greatly influence the corn trade of the world.

In speaking of these successful strides made by England in raising the agriculture of India, we cannot omit mentioning that Russia, too, had the intention of imitating her British rival, and began, nearly ten years ago, to dig a canal from the Yaxartes river to the so-called Hungry Steppe. The work was initiated with a great deal of fuss, but, owing to the embezzlements committed by the officers entrusted with it, it soon turned out a failure. The pockets of the officers may have been satiated, but the Steppe is as *hungry* as ever it was.

Where, in spite of the efforts of the Government, natural calamities have frustrated the work of the agriculturist, and the country has been visited by famine, the Government has, on every occasion, put forth signal efforts for alleviation, and has thereby done much good to the suffering people. From 1873 to 1879, several districts have been visited by the terrible plague of famine. We then saw the touching spectacle of how the Christian inhabitants of the distant west, namely, the people of England, hastened to succour their starving brethren in the distant Brahminic and Moslem East. To the appeal of the English Press, thousands and thousands responded by voluntary contribution; the Lord Mayor of London put himself at the head of the movement, and the sums collected on two occasions alone amounted to nearly one million sterling. It may be well imagined what moral effect this assistance had upon the fanatic Mohammedans of India, who, in a similar case, would have refused to give even a farthing to the Christian sufferer. The Government performed its part by undertaking an extraordinary variety of useful works, by employing several millions of persons, by feeding with gratuitous charity several millions more, and by incurring an expenditure which from 1874 to 1879, has been reckoned at the grand total of sixteen millions sterling.

In turning to the enlightenment given to the

natives of India by their foreign rulers, we may fairly state that education and literature were hardly ever patronised by the native rulers, in the time of their greatest glory, to such an extent as we find to-day under the foreign Christian conqueror. The Mohammedans may well boast that their prophet said : "Indulge in learning from the cradle to the grave," or, "Go after science, be it even at the frontier of China;" but I can assure my readers that learning and science never enjoyed at the hands of Mohammedan princes that extraordinary care our theoretical students, buried in their libraries, are so anxious to discover in some of the great princes of the Mohammedan world. Their learning and science chiefly consisted of theology, grammar, and scholastic speculation, and was the common property of a very restricted number of men; whilst the learning and science patronised by the representatives of our culture in India, aims at the diffusion of light amongst the larger masses, prints books and tracts for the people, and, by raising the standard of intelligence, strikes a deadly blow at the distinctions of caste and rank.

The educational system carried on through primary and normal schools, and the three universities of Calcutta, Madras, and Bombay, costs the Government of India annually the sum of £800,000,

or about one-fortieth part of the net available revenue.
There are 65,500 institutions, including schools and
colleges of all sorts, and the number of students
amounts to nearly two millions, out of which 72,200
are girls, at schools maintained for them especially.
This number of school-attending children is certainly
not very large, for it shows only nine scholars to a
thousand of the population; but where do we find, in
the Mohammedan world, a similar average percentage,
and what is the number of Bashkir, Kazan-Tartar, and
Tschuvashian students, supported by Russia, when
compared with the above percentage? Observe, besides, that out of these colleges and universities supported by the British Government issues annually a
large number of natives, conversant not only with .
English literature, but also with various branches of
the modern sciences : and to find a swarthy-looking
Asiatic quoting Shakespeare, Virgil, and Homer, is
an extraordinary but not unusual spectacle. With
regard to literature, we must mention that many
valuable works, on History, *Belles-Lettres*, nay, even
on Mohammedan and Brahminic theology, have been
published at the expense of the Government in the
native languages. In the course of only one year
4,900 have been published, of which 550 are in
English, 3,050 in the vernacular, 7,730 in the clas-
sical langages of India, and 570 in more than one

language. Finally, let us add that vernacular news-
papers, freely discussing and criticising the governmental and political affairs of the country, are increasing and spreading from day to day, and almost
begin to vie, in their free and unrestrained language,
with the press of the English mother-country. Their
number amounts to several hundreds, and their circulation to several hundred thousand copies.

We shall conclude the comparison between the
Russian and English civilising efforts, by alluding to
the great facilities and rapidity afforded in locomotion through the construction of railways in India.
The total length of the lines amounted in 1873 to
5,671, in 1880 to 8,611, and in 1883 to 10,317 miles,
an immense net of railways spanning the Peninsula
in every direction, the capital expended upon which
amounts to beyond two hundred millions sterling,
part of it belonging to the guaranteed companies,
part to the Government, and one part to the native
States. It is true the English themselves profit most
by the railways, inasmuch as they can use the various
lines for strategical purposes, and in developing the
trade of India; but there accrues no less benefit to
the natives themselves, enabled as they are to travel
at fares that I may say are the cheapest in the whole
world.

Considering the vast amount of comforts given to

the natives for the taxes they have to pay to the
Government, we must say that the idea prevailing
throughout all Europe that Great Britain is impover-
ishing India, and getting rich by it, is preposterous
from beginning to end. If we take, for example, the
data furnished by Sir Richard Temple, we shall find
that the ordinary revenue and receipts amounted in
1880 to something like sixty-seven millions, whilst
the ordinary expenditure has risen to sixty-seven and
a half and sixty-six and three-quarter millions during
the years 1879–80 and 1880–81.   It is therefore
ridiculous to surmise, as the enemies of England do,
that the exchequer of the State gets annually a large
surplus from the Indian finances.   What England
gets from India we shall speak of in the next chapter ;
but here we have only intended to draw a comparison
between the ways and means the two representatives
of our western culture in Asia have hitherto employed to spread the era of a better civilisation, and
to diffuse amongst Orientals the idea that the result
of our conquests, though based upon the superiority
of material strength, is to confer upon mankind
in the distant East the true blessings of our better
civilisation, which we are so justly proud of.   In
Russia the people, also subdued by the superiority
of strength, are either disappearing entirely, or
linger in a miserable existence under the horrid

abuses, tyranny, and disorder of utterly corrupt Russian officials, and the dawn of a better era is still hidden in the far future; whilst "the mass of the teeming Indian population desire nothing so much as that sort of repose which they enjoy under the strong, mild, and just rule of England, where every man gathers in quiet the fruits of his toil, is not forced to render up his good against his will, sleeps without fear of violence, has redress for wrongs done to him by his neighbour, performs his religious rites, and follows his caste observances undisturbed, and lifts his eyes towards the State as to a father."

I ask, therefore, can any sober-minded, honest European still doubt as to whom he ought to give preference in the work of civilising Asia? and is it not a shame that the various nations of Europe, influenced by petty rivalries and national vanities, are often blinded to such an extent as to extol Russia at the expense of England?

Where the sacred cause of humanity is involved, there one's views ought not to be confined to national limits; they ought to soar beyond, and honestly try to lift themselves up to the mental and moral attitude which ensures the largest and broadest look-out. As long as the national idea is most forward in the struggle for civilisation, which I consider identical with humanity, it is worthy of the devotion of every true man; but from the moment that, forgetful of its glorious task, the idea becomes pernicious, assailing the noble object of civilisation it once struggled for and defended, I exclaim—" Perish such an idea; let national lines be obliterated, if they are nought but barriers upon which unblushing egotism and unreasoning enmity between nation and nation are inscribed."

I allude, in speaking thus, to the ignominious behaviour of a certain portion of the German and French Press during the late differences between England and Russia in Central Asia—to certain writers who, forgetful of the glorious work hitherto done by England in Asia, were already exulting with triumph at the prospect of what they thought the near end of Great Britain, and, extolling semi-barbarous and despotic Russia, were ready to destroy the *prestige* of the very nation whose banner has always been, and is, the harbinger of a new and better world in the distant regions of the East, and whose shores have proved hitherto the safest asylum of Frenchmen and Germans persecuted for political ideas.

CHAPTER XII.

FROM the comparison we drew in the foregoing chapter between the doings of Russia and Great Britain in Asia, it has become obviously patent that England's position in India must enlist the interest of every European from a humanitarian point of view, and it is, therefore, our duty to support, to the best of our abilities, that agency which most faithfully represents our Western culture, and which, as the real embodiment of what we call *Europeanism*, is best fitted for the onerous but glorious task of spreading in future also, the light of our Western civilisation, to which we intend to convert the masses of Asiatics who are still groaning under the yoke of an old and effete epoch. Moreover, I would bring home the conviction to all Englishmen that they have to persevere in the ambition of their forefathers, and are, so to say, in honour bound to retain India, the field of their civilising action during more than a hundred years.

I may be laughed at for speaking of a *necessity* at a time when the struggle for retention is in preparation. But my insinuation is not so groundless as it seems to be, for I had abundant cause to notice that, in spite of the zeal and enthusiasm for the national honour prevailing amongst a large portion of the British public, there still is a considerable fraction with whom the idea of the possession of India is a matter of utter indifference—a fraction which has invented the famous saying, " Perish India "—and which goes even so far as to be delighted to " see burst" that horrid beast called the British lion. The origin of this rather extraordinary sentiment—what I would style a mental aberration—may be easily discovered, if we view the extraordinary struggle for daily life going on in the densely-peopled island, where the division of wealth and property is so very uneven, and where the preponderating poorer classes are naturally led into such arguments as : What need they care about the prosperity, well-being, and enlightenment of distant races, when help and assistance are so urgently wanted at home; and, more than that, why should the taxes extorted from them be spent upon the prosecution of an imperial policy, by which, as they very unjustly remark, only the upper ten thousand are profiting? These arguments, the outflow of ultra-Liberal or Radical tendencies, have been variously supported by the views of statesmen who, over-confident in the industrial and commercial prosperity of the United Kingdom, were short-sighted enough to maintain that England can stand by itself alone, and that she does not want colonies at all for her natural greatness.

Now, in order to prove the utter fallacy of such theories, it will be quite sufficient to draw the attention of the reader to the great advantages England derives from her Indian possessions . through her commercial connections and shipping; connections which are continually increasing, so that out of the 154,000,000 sterling at which the total trade of India was valued, the lion's share fell decidedly to England.

"The total exports of British produce from the United Kingdom are valued at £240,000,000 a year; the total value of our exports of British produce to India is £32,000,000, *i.e.,* more than one-eighth. This sum does not include £6,000,000 of treasure, and £3,000,000 of foreign produce, which gives employment to our shipping, though it does not give work to our manufactories. £32,000,000, therefore, represents the amount of English goods for which we find a market in India. That is, it is worth £5,000,000 more to us than the United States, and a third again as much as Australia.

"The most important articles of this trade are

cottons, metals, machinery, railway plant, woollen goods, and coal. Of these, cotton is the most valuable. In 1882–83 our whole export of cotton from Lancashire was worth £76,000,000; of that India took £25,000,000, that is, India is worth as a customer to Lancashire half as much as all the rest of the world put together. Of the next importance is the metal trade, worth £6,000,000. This includes cutlery from Sheffield and Birmingham, and copper from Swansea. Next, machinery; of this we sent £1,750,000, chiefly from Leeds, Manchester, and Glasgow. Next, railway plant, valued at £1,500,000, chiefly from Leeds, Middlesbrough, Sheffield, Birmingham, Barrow, and Bristol. The trade in woollen is worth £1,250,000 to the West Riding of Yorkshire, and the coal trade £1,000,000." (Professor Cyril Ransome, "Our Colonies and India," London, 1885.)

The profits derived in this way do not certainly form a contemptible portion of the wealth of Great Britain, and I am really curious to know where and how the much boasted-of industrial and commercial activity of Great Britain would find a market, if India did belong to any other Power of Europe. It would be sufficient to allude to the fact that, from the time Russia took possession of the Central Asian khanates, the English trade through Afghanistan to Bokhara has greatly diminished, and the exorbitantly

N

prohibitive duties introduced by Russia may well result in entirely locking out British trade from the
country beyond the Oxus, as well as from northern
Persia. Tea, cotton, and iron-wares, have been almost
totally supplanted by Russian articles in the same
line, and there is no exaggeration in assuming that
every move of the Northern colossus towards the
south is a blow to British trade and industry.

Besides the commercial benefits, we may well
take into account the appointments and salaries drawn
by Englishmen in the Indian Service, as well as the
pensions they obtain, after a comparatively short
service, from the Exchequer of India, and which,
with few exceptions, is spent in the insular home.
The number of covenanted Civil Service officers in
India amounts to nearly one thousand, and the
number of those European officials who are termed
uncovenanted, employed as railway and telegraph
officials, in the medical department, etc., is still more
considerable, and if we add to these the 4,570 com-
missioned officers, we shall get a good number of
those Britons who, in no small degree, contribute to
English wealth by spending the hard-earned Indian
savings in their British homes. Last, not least, we
would point out the immensely large sums of English
capital invested in Indian railways, irrigation canals,
and other concerns, and, particularly, the thousands

of English merchants, owners of mills, manufacturers of indigo and tea plantations, of shipping, etc., who work the country in every direction for the benefit of British capital; and the inference is glaringly self-evident that the possession of India is not to be trifled with, and that a loss of this dependency would be a deadly blow to the British nation and State.

In passing to the moral standing Great Britain enjoys through her Indian possessions, I shall begin with pointing to the respect and consideration the British conquests in the distant East have secured to our whole European world, and to our Christian civilisation in general, among all the inhabitants of Asia. The name of *Feringhi*, *i.e.*, European, by which Englishmen are known in India, China, Persia, and Tartary as far as Tobolsk, has obtained a lustre unparalleled, hitherto, in the history of mankind, and I very much doubt whether the name of *Rum*, by which the old Romans were known in these outlying regions of the Asiatic world, could ever boast of the splendour enjoyed by the name of *Feringhi*. The conquest of India has ever been the *ne plus ultra* of political might and power of the Asiatics; it was the radiant gem in the crown of Djenghis, Timur, and Nadir; and, quite recently, it has become the light which has dazzled the eyes of the Eastern peoples, for whenever I heard in my

N 2

lonely wanderings the greatness of the West extolled, the instance quoted always was, that the Feringhis have overthrown the throne of the Mogul, and have become possessors of the proverbial treasures of India. The moral *prestige* of this conquest was, therefore, of almost equal importance with the introduction of steam navigation on the waters of eastern Asia, for it struck terror into the hearts of China, Japan, and the whole of eastern Asia, and has greatly contributed to our supremacy in those parts of the world. To these moral achievements belong, besides, the services the English have rendered, and are still rendering, to European science, by having opened a large store of information regarding the history, the languages, and the archæology of India. Without the valuable works of William Jones, Richardson, Horace Hayman Wilson, John Muir, Monier Williams, and a great many others, we could hardly pursue our Persian and Sanscrit studies in the way we are now enabled to do, for they have laid the foundation of our modern investigations, just as the valuable publications in Oriental literature made by Alexander Korosy de Csoma, Sprenger, Nassau Lees, Raverty, Prinsep, Fergusson, and others, would have been impossible without the assistance of the Anglo-Indian Government; and, finally, it was the English standing in India which has enabled us to study the adjacent countries—nay, to get acquainted with the past and present of nearly half Asia.

It is, therefore, in consideration of the strictly and purely humanitarian part which England plays in India, that every European must feel a lively interest in the maintenance of British rule in India. He must be convinced of the indisputable fact that, with the retreat of the English from that peninsula, either the most horrible anarchy will ensue, and rapine, bloodshed, and murder take the place of the present settled, and peaceful condition of the country —for India was never able to govern herself—or that the barbarous despotism of Russia will inaugurate a new era of Asiatic disorders, and sweep away every trace of that glorious building erected through the skill, perseverance, and heroism of England.

It may be that, at a distant future, the various populations of India, gradually getting sufficiently trained in the principles of self-government, and acquiring the necessary notions of our Western culture, may do without the leading strings indispensable for the present, and may be able to stand on their own feet. I say such a time may come, and must come : but then the pupil will separate from its master, not with blood-stained hands, but on the most friendly terms, and the relations between the conqueror and the conquered will naturally change into affectionate memory and ties of intimate friendship. But since that time is, as I said, a good way off, Englishmen must look with pride at the task still before them. They have done half of the work only, and they must not shrink from the responsibility and trouble of doing the other half. The deep sense of duty, a special heritage of the English nation, handed down to them from the days of their Puritan ancestors, has made them scorn the idea of holding rule over others solely to benefit themselves. This feeling—I use the words of Professor Ransome—has never been stronger than at the present day; and, I may add, that I hope it will retain its strength in upholding her beneficial rule over India for many, many generations to come.

In order to effect this purpose, it is of urgent necessity that a great change should take place in the minds of the English people concerning their views on the value of India. Before all, it is that ominous and disastrous indifference, coupled with unpardonable ignorance in matters connected with India, which must decidedly give way to a lively interest and to a continuous care for this question of national importance. The nation at large must be penetrated by the glory of its position, and ought not to shrug shoulders when India, Afghanistan, and Central Asia become the topics of public discussion.

During the twenty-two years that I have been

connected with the literature of this political question, and whilst on my various lecturing tours in every direction of the United Kingdom, I was always astonished and painfully surprised upon seeing how little the British public at large cares about India, and what inadequate proportion the authorities bear to the importance of the question. The number of those who formerly busied themselves with a thorough investigation of Central Asia has of late fearfully diminished in England; no wonder that criminal indifference was rapidly spreading, and that astute Russia, making the best of this English national mistake, could easily progress on her way, and feigning amity could, with the assassin's dagger concealed from view, steadily approach unwary England. I am sure that, from the moment when Englishmen will cease to discuss the question whether India ought to be given up or retained, and when solid watchfulness will displace the present apathy, then the position of Great Britain in India and throughout all Asia will change at once. Russia, her great and most formidable rival, will see that the period of constant trumperies is at an end, that she will have to face, henceforward, not the whimsical views of party politicians, but the will of a great and mighty nation, a nation jealous of its honour, and ready to defend her banner with all her available resources.

CHAPTER XIII.

To speak of one self is, according to an Oriental saying, "the business of the devil." It is, indeed, a most
unpleasant business, and if I do it nevertheless, I
feel actuated by motives I cannot leave unexplained
on the present occasion. The position of a foreigner,
coming forward to defend the interests of a country
not his own, of a people to whom he is an alien, is
certainly a very rare occurrence in the history of
political literature and politics in general. I do not
wonder at all to see myself accused as a fanatic, as
a maniac, as a man whose fancy is totally incomprehensible, and for whose doings people could find
the only explanation in his Hungarian nationality, a
view which I frequently found expressed in the
following sentence :—" Professor Vambéry is a Hungarian, carrying in his breast, in indelible characters,
hatred of Russia. He cannot forget 1848, when
General Paskievitch compelled his countrymen to lay
down their arms raised against Austria. He is con-

tinually brooding revenge, and thence his constant
efforts to embroil us with Russia." Well, I dare to say
this supposition is utterly false. I entered the arena
of political discussion, as I have already stated else-
where, from motives strictly humanitarian, and I
am in no way influenced either by my national
feelings involving antipathies against Russia, or by
any special predilection for, or unconditional admiration of the English. I have been often taken to task
as to why I cared as a student, and as a professor of
Oriental languages, for politics in general; politics
which lie outside the sphere of a strictly theoretical
man, and may be called quite an out of the way
occupation for anybody whose attention is supposed
to be absorbed by languages, history, and ethnology.
My answer has always been, and is even now, that
there is a great difference between the student who
spends his life in his library, viewing things from
a distance, and the traveller, who moves on the
field of practical experience, and who, assuredly, is
more vividly impressed by what he hears and sees
around him. The traveller lives and breathes for a
long time, if not during his whole life, *with* the
peoples and nations he came across in his journeys,
and whom he has made the special subject of his
inquiries. He likes to indulge in speculations about
their future; he is eagerly bent upon ameliorating

their condition; and as the future of such nations is intimately connected with the daily question of European politics, the traveller is, so to say, dragged into the field of political speculation, and cannot help becoming a politician himself.

Similar reasons account for my so-called English sympathies. If an Orientalist cannot be prevented from becoming a so-called politician, he should not be censured for following in his political lines the principle of true liberty, and from paying his tribute of admiration to that portion of the European world which he finds to be at the top of our civilisation, and where he perceives all those qualities and conditions which constitute the purest and most perfect light of our western culture. There may be, and there no doubt are, nations more deeply versed in abstruse learning, more peaceful, and more imaginative than the English; but there certainly is none so free and independent in their private and in public life. None can boast of those liberal institutions, none of being able to appreciate so thoroughly the value of individual and independent action in private concerns and in public affairs. Now, I cannot help saying that, with me, liberty and freedom is the highest sign of perfection; and not only do I expect the free man to show an earnest zeal to liberate others, but I consider such a man to be the most

appropriate instrument for accomplishing that purpose. Only a free man is capable of great deeds;
only he can wipe out the superstitions and vices of
decaying Asia; and for these reasons it is that my
sympathies are with the English, whose superior
manhood, fearlessness and self-respect, enables them
to carry through the regeneration of Asia more
successfully than any of the European nations
extant.

I need scarcely say that these sympathies of mine
do not interfere with my forming a fair judgment on
the drawbacks of the English character, drawbacks
which are of little or no harm at all in their doings
in Asia, and may at most be an impediment to their
internal progress, a state of things which I feel I
have neither the right nor the ability to criticise, and
which will always remain outside the pale of my
political writings.

It is in connection with this view that I found it
rather absurd to see myself classified by certain people
as belonging to the Conservative party. I have
nothing to do with party politics in England, and
the only reason for seeing myself identified with the
interests of this party may be found in the circumstance that this party has of late years shown a more
pronounced tendency to support the Imperial policy;
it has manifested greater zeal for the maintenance of

those foreign possessions which constitute the glory of English enterprise, and has shown greater skill and superior statesmanship in the preservation of the *prestige* of Great Britain all over the globe. This party may, therefore, be styled more British, more manly, and more active in the service of humanity abroad than the other party, which, for reasons I do not care to inquire into here, has greatly injured England's standing abroad, and has got decidedly an unlucky hand in foreign affairs. This disproportion in success is, I think, quite sufficient to turn anybody interested in England's successes in Asia to the party of more active and luckier politicians, and this is my sole reason for siding with the Conservatives and with their policy in Asia.

I suppose it was this false supposition that has exposed me, during the last year, so frequently to the attacks of over-zealous Liberals, and has subjected my writings to sundry misinterpretations. Whilst, in former years, I had attracted the ill-will of such Continental writers only as, blinded by their hatred of England, have rushed at me with all kinds of invectives and imputations, I had of late the rare luck of getting hits from the other side of the Channel too, partly in the so-called Liberal Press, partly in private letters sent to me to Buda Pesth. As an old writer, I am not at all sensitive to the asperity of criticism, on the contrary, I greatly enjoy it, and, in order to show to the reader some specimens of these effusions of Liberal tenderness, I beg leave to publish two of those epistles :—

"LONDON, *9th Feb.*, 1880.

"To PROFESSOR VAMBÉRY,

"The University, Buda Pesth.

" SIR,—Being, I presume, a blasted Austrian or Hungarian, I can understand your sympathy with the *manly, energetic,* and *wise* policy of this Government. At the same time, I should advise you to keep your advice to yourself with regard to the British policy in Asia, as although, no doubt, you are very clever, thank God we have in this country men who are, perhaps, as far-seeing as you make yourself out to be.

" Yours obediently,

"A. R."

———————————————

" *3rd April,* 1885.

" PROFESSOR VAMBÉRY.

("Please note.—You cannot truthfully deny anything here stated in your lectures, as you are supported by the *Jingonastic Conservatives*.)

" SIR,—Did it ever occur to you that the English people (all classes) can best form an opinion on the so-called dispute between England and Russia without the aid of a foreigner to assist them, as it is a quarter of a century since you travelled in some of those parts ?

" What would the Hungarian people think of an Englishman giving them advice—even by a lecture—if Hungary had a dispute with another country ? Even we can see through it—the old hatred of the old Hungarians towards Russia because of her aid to Austria to keep your country united to her. There is no war fever in this country by the great bulk of the people except what is kept up by a certain class of Press-writers to certain papers who represent the upper class, who are interested with India, and now hold up Russia as a 'bogey.' Even your Mr. Marvin is a well-known alarmist, and is of no age to have any practical experience, although he sets himself up to be even as great an authority as Lord Granville, our great Foreign Minister. Why, it is only four years ago we killed and wounded 5,000 Afghans, and attempted to annex a large part of their kingdom. Russia had good excuse then to complain far more than we now about this debatable land, which, you know, is not inhabited by Afghans, but by Turkomans.

" In fact, black as you paint Russia in your lecture, it is white compared with our English annexations and aggression in the various states forming India. Read the conquest of India by the East India Company, and afterwards under the English Crown.

" This India is no good to the industrial classes of this country—it is a receiving house for appointments for the Upper Ten to all kinds of positions. The parties you lecture to, they are only a class in this country, and not the people at large. It was only a short time ago we had to advance India £200,000 to assist her after the famine.

" Yours respectfully,

" W. R."

Such flattering testimonials of my political activity, in England, are perhaps very little of an encouraging nature, and I can easily imagine how delighted my Russian friends will be in reading these acknowledgments received for my services. But I can afford them the consolation that these outbursts of fanaticism, coming as they do mostly from over-

heated brains, are scarcely worth noticing, considering
the really undeserved approval I have met with for
the last twenty years at the hands of a large majority
of the indulgent British public. It was particularly
my last lecturing tour in England which has given
me the full conviction that my various writings,
although derided in certain quarters and at certain
periods, have not fallen to the ground. The warning
voice which I have raised at various times, when a
seemingly cloudless sky deluded the intentionally careless crowd of politicians, has not echoed away, but left
an impression on the minds of a few thinking Englishmen. My gratitude to them is boundless; it is
owing to this gratitude that I undertook to write the
present book, which, destined for a larger circulation,
will, I fondly hope, rouse the masses also to the
necessity of an active, patriotic, and decisive policy
as to Russia.

And lastly, it is this feeling of thankfulness
which animates me to go on as before, unflinchingly,
in the path of my political writing.

By doing so I am in hopes to achieve two purposes—one, to draw the attention of Europe in
general, to the excessive increase of the power of
barbarous and despotic Russia; a power obtained
through the connivance of our miserable diplomacy,
and fraught with dangers to the liberal institutions of

all Europe. In looking around amongst the European nations to discover the one fittest to form an effective barrier against this ruthless aggression, I found that Germany still wants a good deal of time before she matures into such a manhood as to come forward as the real defender of liberty; and that France, being a large room full of *enfants gâtés*, offers less security to the sacred cause of liberty, owing to the fickle minds and puerile freaks of her citizens. It is only the solid rock of Anglo-Saxon character which will furnish the necessary material for effective bulwarks; and my second purpose in view is, therefore, to strengthen this national element, as far as it lies in the power of a writer; to animate the English to maintain their position in Asia, which is inseparably connected with their power in Europe. If I have in the least succeeded in my aspirations to that effect, I shall deem myself abundantly rewarded.

INDEX.

o

PRINTED BY CASSELL & COMPANY, LIMITED, LA BELLE SAUVAGE, LONDON, E.C.